Andy Neal & Dio

CREATIVITY

BEGINS

WITH

YOU

31 practical workshops to explore
your creative potential

Laurence King

First published in Great Britain in 2022 by

Laurence King Student & Professional
An imprint of Quercus Editions Ltd
Carmelite House
50 Victoria Embankment
London EC4Y 0DZ

An Hachette UK company

A CIP catalogue record for this book is available
from the British Library

TPB ISBN 978-1-52942-022-7
EBOOK ISBN 978-1-52942-023-4

10 9 8 7 6 5 4 3 2 1

Design by Blok Graphic, London

Printed and bound in China by C&C Printing., Ltd.

creativitybeginswithyou.co.uk

LAURENCE KING

Contents

Introduction

Another book on creativity – really?

Think about where you come from. Who you are. Your interests. What drives you, and the people or things that make you come alive. Consider your previous creative experience (or lack of). Your personality. Your ego. You the introvert. You the extrovert. Your visual, auditory and kinaesthetic learning preferences, or the profound existential questions that resonate with you. All of these things (and many, many more) position you as a one-of-a-kind, creative powerhouse that needs winding up and setting in motion.

The majority of us spend more time consuming than creating, yet creative expression is essential for us all – to the point that our happiness depends on it. To view creativity as innate talent or as a superpower only present in certain 'artistic' individuals is a mistake. Those of us in the creative industries – the so-called professionals – may be more practised at applying our creative intuition, but everyone has the capacity for creativity, and nurturing your creative abilities constitutes a core component of your overall growth as a person.

Backstory

Our shared interest in creativity and creative processes evolved from our own education and the environment that was the traditional British art school. We both benefitted from tutors who revelled in provocation, who would push, challenge and encourage us way beyond what felt comfortable. The result was a growing fascination with the question of *why* (rather than *what*), and the creative journey itself became more important than the destination. This became evident both in the development of our own work and in what we observed of the underlying processes of the artists and designers we admired. Over time, outcomes became a by-product of a process of exploration that was far more interesting, so it was no real surprise that we both ended up working in education – where questions are often more prevalent than answers. Getting inside the head of a student to help them untangle their thinking was far more satisfying than any final solution to a given problem. The outcome would grow old; the learning would last forever. The making, the journey, the wrestling and tension is, for us, where the real action is – *design* as a verb, rather than a noun.

Over the past decade, this interest has developed into a more overt pursuit of understanding the place of creativity and process in our teaching, which has led to workshops seeking to frame each student's working methodology as the main event, rather than considering their process as a means to an end. What if the way you worked as a designer, or writer, or architect became the object of self-study – exploring something more profound than the pursuit of developing a logo, or story, or building? What would you notice? What would surprise or shock you? What would you want to change or protect?

Creativity Begins with You started as a series of informal learning experiments with design students. We pooled our collective observations to that point, and invited individuals to reflect on their existing practice and to propose alternative versions of their future selves. Over time, the experiments grew and developed into a body of work that seemed to have an emerging centre of gravity. There was a constellation of creative possibilities surrounding every student's practice, and the sessions sought to empower and equip them with an ever-expanding pool of materials and methods to refer to whenever they felt stuck, uninspired or hindered by self-doubt.

The material in this book is, therefore, part practical workshop, part provocative guide, part theoretical conversation, and is based on our experiences and observations from those early experiments onwards. Just as there can never be enough songs (or novels, or typefaces, or paintings) in the world, this book seeks to add to the conversation around creativity in a way that places you in the middle of the picture, working outwards from there.

Growth

We started writing this book with an underlying belief that creativity is not primarily something we *learn*; it is something we *are*. We are often taught (albeit indirectly) that creativity is something you either have or don't have, and this forms a belief that has a significant bearing on our ability to function creatively in the long term; many people will write themselves off simply because they were told they couldn't draw at school. If you can take the step of trusting that you are inherently creative, regardless of how you feel, you can then learn practices and principles that will encourage and grow your ability for creativity. You may have further to travel than the seasoned professional, but know that you're already on the road, with an innate capacity to move.

Creativity is a generative behaviour that springs from a unique combination of factors directly hardwired to our identity. It looks different from person to person, and it evolves as we grow. Our emphasis, therefore, is not so much on your capacity to learn something – it's on the conditions and environments that shape what's already there. If you fundamentally believe that you're not creative, you have established an immovable mountain that you will have no ambition even to begin to climb. Similarly, if you do believe you are (to a greater or lesser degree) creative but spend huge amounts of energy trying to be *more so*, you're probably asking the wrong questions and needlessly exhausting yourself.

For many of us, however (and despite our combined efforts over the last century to capture what 'it' is), creativity still sits more comfortably in the unknowable realm – a mystery. It's something we live out day by day, as an extension of life seen from a unique perspective, which goes some way to explaining why we have such a hard time tying it down.

There is a mystery to creativity that needs to remain, to a certain degree, undefined. By looking too closely or explaining too thoroughly, there's a danger of dismantling the very thing we're trying to observe. Catch a butterfly and pin it to a board to marvel

'You must not trample on other people's secret gardens. You must remember: to suggest is to create; to describe is to destroy.'

Robert Doisneau [1]

> 'People have always referred to the arts to express that which could not be explained. And therein lies the real power of art and design. Artists and designers have the ability and the sensory vocabulary to express rather than explain. We, therefore, are in a position to engage with an audience on a very deep, essentially human level.'

Stefan Boufler [2]

at its beauty, and you kill the essence of what you were drawn to. That said, if we never attempt to comprehend what we don't understand, we'll endlessly repeat ourselves and never grow. Finding the balance between the mystery and the understanding is where the magic lies and – we hope – forms the heart of this book.

You at the centre

Encouraging creativity in others has, over the past decade, become our primary concern, and shaping our teaching activity around the needs of the individual has allowed us to nurture that creativity more effectively. In order for us to do this, it's vital to identify the unique characteristics, needs and behaviours of that individual (the context of their creativity), and to recognize how and why certain conditions or environments can support, nourish or even challenge their creative growth.

Creativity Begins with You explores these themes in three dedicated chapters – Identity, Habit and Play – which go some way in helping to define those internal and external characteristics more clearly. We then conclude with the definitive fourth and final chapter, Practice, which feeds your intellectual growth by way of more than 30 hands-on workshops for you to explore at your leisure.

Why does this all matter?

We believe exploring our creativity is essential for several reasons – not least that the world would be far more utilitarian if it weren't for our collective endeavours.

There is an ease with which our creativity can become blunted through use, and there is a constant need for us to re-question and re-evaluate our assumptions and practice.

In his book *On Directing Film*, David Mamet says that 'the conscious mind always wants to be liked and wants to be interesting … the conscious mind is going to suggest the obvious, the cliché, because these things offer the security of having succeeded in the past.'[3] The pressures of continual measurement and assessment in the educational world, and the weight of commercial deadlines, economic bias or self-doubt can cause us to fall back on tried-and-tested routes or creative patterns. We play to our historic strengths and end up producing safe yet mostly uninteresting work (or no work at all). In doing so, we can end up like a cover band of old projects, continually replaying our favourite hits, and slowly sucking the soul from the work we once loved. There is an ease with which our creativity can become blunted through use, and there is a constant need for us to re-question and re-evaluate our assumptions and practice.

Creativity within the education sector is experiencing broader change. With fewer arts subjects being available to the under 18s, there is a concerning shift in the traditional art-student demographic. The ongoing commercialization of education (university courses as products, and students as customers) and aggressive adoption of data-driven business models has changed the atmosphere of the art school. While much of this change is inevitable and shaped by broader global issues, the impact on our long-term creative development (and our ability to learn) is compromised. When we become numbers in a system, our individuality can be lost and, as we will explore, that uniqueness plays a significant role in our creative development.

Whether you are someone who's never considered themselves creative or interesting enough, a student entering art school or university, or even a seasoned practitioner with decades of experience, there is always more to learn. Never has there been such a time to re-focus on the individual nature of the creative journey and take ownership of your own learning.

So yes, another book on creativity, but this one is specifically about yours.

Identity

Chapter 1:

Identity

'There are at least two major tasks to human life. The first task is to build a strong "container" or identity; the second is to find the contents that the container was meant to hold.'

Richard Rohr.[1]

Introduction

Our formative years in education shape many of us in a particular way, essentially rooting us in a worldview that generally assumes there's a right and a wrong way of doing things. Choices are often presented as black or white, as nature or nurture, left wing or right wing, true or false, and these dualistic views can create a conceptual division in the way we think about everything – including creativity. This is important because most of us would agree that a central quality of creativity is its capacity to embrace possibility (the grey) and, as such, any dualistic bias can limit our potential to grow creatively. There is a real chance that we naturally polarize creative choices into an either/or scenario (reducing the expansive *possibility* into a reductive *yes* or *no*), without ever being aware of it. If you've ever reflected on your work, thinking 'Is this right?' out of a fear of getting it 'wrong', you're probably thinking dualistically. We all tend to question our work, and that's OK – questions are good. It's what we do with them, however, that's significant in the long term.

In his book *A Year with Swollen Appendices*, artist/producer/writer Brian Eno lists some of the qualities used to identify him: mammal, father, musician, writer, grumbler, drifting clarifier, and so on.[2] There is a sense in his writings that, by not being limited to a singular dualistic boundary ('I am this, I am not that'), he is somehow free to be more fully who he is ('I am greater than the sum of my parts'... Aristotle.[3]). Eno is an artist *and* a producer *and* a writer (and many other things). Rob Bell, author, speaker, pastor (and many other things), takes this idea further and talks about the integration of all our disparate qualities: 'Holism is the reality that emerges only when all the parts are put together but can't be individually located, labeled, or identified at a smaller, component, parts level.'[4] Education itself, particularly at undergraduate level, is guilty – at least in part – to a narrowing of our focus. Subjects are presented (often for the benefit of potential students) in neatly packaged bundles that define a curated pattern of study – increasingly focused towards a specific career, and inevitably to the exclusion of other practices and processes. Even if your creativity is located around a particular discipline (graphic design, for example), limiting yourself to that label means some things are in and others are out.

However, we are far more than the labels we place upon each other. And, even more than the unifying qualities of holism, where we begin to see the relationship between constituent parts of the whole *us*, if we seek to remove the idea of labels altogether, a refreshing process of creative rediscovery can begin. If you choose to see your creative practice (your *process*) as part of a unique, one-of-a-kind perspective – holistically linked to who you are – you'll value and invest in that process at a far deeper and more primal level. We normally place a high value on any species surviving in small numbers (protecting rare orchids, sea turtles or indigenous languages), and we generally celebrate diversity in the natural world. Yet so often, our understanding, and teaching, of creativity can be a top-down transference of externally imposed and homogenized principles, rather than a journey that seeks to discover, protect and nurture something fragile and unique (one in nearly eight billion, when you come to think about it!). True creativity consists of unearthing and embracing all the factors that make you who you are, and then framing and nurturing those qualities, rather than dictating and forcing others. Aiming for tonal variation, rather than black or white.

So, we want to begin this creative journey by dropping any expectation that there's a right way to make or define things when it comes to your creativity – to encourage you to let go of the black or white, to embrace possibility, and start exploring what *you* bring to the table.

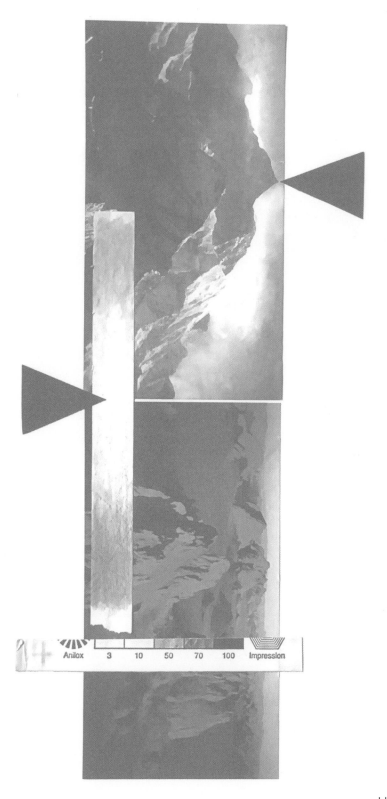

This page: Balance—Distinctive, collage by Tom Jenkins (see page 214 Combine)

This chapter begins to unpack five key themes that we believe are essential when considering your wider creative identity, thereby setting the scene for everything that follows.

There are processes

In writing this book, we are very aware that our backgrounds are within the world of design, which naturally shapes our bias. However, many of the principles of design are, in essence, universal and apply across a broad range of creative disciplines. Common to any established design/creative practice is a *process* – the defined or intuitive model upon which a given individual or organization will base any creative activity. This is often put in place for the benefit of the student (to teach), the client (to market) or finance department (to cost). Indeed, *design process* and *design thinking* are terms regularly used to describe definitive *things* in the current discourse surrounding creativity. The latter is often a misleading term – in most instances, when people refer to design thinking, what they usually mean is one of four things: thinking, creativity, a process or a strategy. Most academic courses in design will have their own unique articulation, which can act as the skeleton around which a richer curriculum is built. This is also true for many well-respected industry bodies internationally.

The danger of frameworks

Design doesn't claim ownership of creativity, but it's perhaps the discipline that has focused the most attention on identifying what creativity is, and on finding ways of communicating it to others. (Do an online image search for *design process diagram* and you will see something of the scale of our combined attempts to capture the essence of a creative process.) The danger is, however, that although any given formula can establish a clear path to work from initially, over time it can create a limiting furrow that ultimately reduces spontaneity, risk and play – key qualities of creativity (which we cover in Chapter 3). We end up following the same routines, using the same examples or words; even our love of a particular discipline can wane if left unchecked. We can also fall foul of the duality trap – assuming that there is, somewhere out there, a perfect way of working.

No single process

We believe that there is no one optimum creative process (and we refer to this in more detail in Chapter 2). There is no single way to *be* creative because we *are* creative by nature. *Being* creative can be tied to a specific expression of that creativity (artist, designer, musician) and this, like dualism, ultimately limits us. Instead, there are processes – in and through and around which we need to operate, and from which we can always continue to learn.

Mystery

The 'perfect process' problem, we think, stems from a deeply rooted desire to articulate a magic formula that will guarantee creative success. However, this desire is ultimately undermined by the limitations of language. We've all seen pictures of the Northern Lights, or footage of killer whales breaching the surface of a mirror-flat Pacific Ocean. You may know of friends who, with only a large elastic band strapped to their ankles, have jumped from bridges in remote parts of New Zealand, or busy professionals who choose to spend their vacations nursing orphaned babies in some of the poorest parts of the world. We can imagine what it must be like, and their verbal or written descriptions will often come pretty close, but the experience itself will almost certainly leave the individual lost for words. And it's not just the high-octane, extreme activities that cause us to run out of adjectives or allegories. Simple observations, like watching the morning light dance through the trees, or sitting down to a well-earned cup of tea, or seeing a friend come out of their shell after a period of personal difficulty, all carry something of the sublime and ultimately have to be experienced rather than described.

Some things (auroras, orcas, adrenaline, compassion, light, tea, hope...) can go beyond our capacity to understand; we're only able to share that experience in real time. The essence of these encounters needs to be celebrated as *mystery* – beyond our capacity to know or make sense of, only to be explained through experience. By extension, we'd argue that the very act of nurturing and shaping a creative idea – in whatever form this may take – carries something of this mystery with it. In our pursuit of the perfect process, there's a danger that we forget the place of creative mystery and become driven by our need to understand and define, rather than to experience.

By focusing on your unique creativity as the thing of greatest value – rather than the outcomes you create – you can begin to redefine how you engage with new ideas, and develop a deep-rooted need to bring them to life.

Processes

We have all utilized creative methods, diagrams or models in some way; formal education is essentially built upon them. They are helpful and form a good foundation from which to develop. However, moving beyond a formula – or indeed, beyond the notion that any of these diagrams or descriptions are correct – is fundamental to a deeper level of creative growth. In the same way that moving from a single title (father, or husband, or designer, or teacher) and embracing them all holistically (father and husband and...) can bring a degree of personal freedom, moving from *process* (singular) to *processes* (plural) seems to unlock something at the core of how you function creatively. Arguably a modest shift in the use of our (limited) language, but our observations have been that this particular adjustment in thinking opens up a significant number of new creative possibilities. What if I worked like this? What if I changed that? What if I stopped this? What if I started that? What if...? Utilizing processes seems to fuel any existing dualistic thinking far less – perhaps because there is far less room for comparison. Journey and destination are held on an equal footing.

You are distinctive

We each have a unique story to tell. Where we come from, who and what shaped our development, our wiring and interests, and how we continue to evolve in an ever-changing world is, for want of a better description, extraordinary. Culturally, however, conventions exist that categorize some stories as better than others, or propose that some actions, opinions or creations matter more than others.

Thoughts on value

Our experiences working with students suggest that this value perspective is driven by a broader worldview that fundamentally works against your creative self – essentially proposing that what you achieve is more important than who you are. Celebrity. Status. Notoriety. Fame. Money. Power. Scale. Volume... These are all external rewards that prompt our creative gaze to focus outwards. Somewhere else. Something else. Someone else. Short-term, instant gratification. The problem with this worldview is that it causes our wider sense of creative worth to be judged in the same way. The novel that was never published. The design that lost the pitch. The song that didn't get recorded. All failed attempts to succeed in whatever industry you deem relevant and now, by implication, all redundant creative works that reduce your sense of individual worth because they don't endorse celebrity, status, notoriety or whatever. Our default emphasis is often on the perceived success of the outcome, which can, over time, become a paralyzing force if we have a run of 'unsuccessful' ventures – affecting how we subsequently engage with, develop or complete any creative task.

However, if we knew that the unpublished novel was written by a single parent, working three jobs just to break even, and that it took over five years to complete, our view of its unpublished state may be a little less dismissive. We might even be curious to learn what it was about, and we would certainly value it more highly as a creative work – despite its non-published status.

Something interesting begins to happen when we enlarge our field of vision. The context, ambition and arduous creative process (with its inevitable mistakes) significantly increase the value of the whole. The outcome is made stronger by including both the process and the person. By considering a broader set of factors, the lack of a publishing deal is somehow overshadowed by grit, determination, resolve, belief and an undeniable sense of possibility.

We may not all face the challenges of a single parent fighting for the time, space or energy to write. Some of us may be in a far more comfortable, even privileged, position, with time and money to help us *be* creative. *Being* creative may even be our day job. Whatever your situation, though, we believe there's an alternative – more helpful criteria that can create a more fertile environment from which to start thinking about creativity. Integrity. Care. Honesty. Determination. Consequence. Responsibility. Balance. Truth... Importantly, these are mostly internal rewards that make us accountable for our own choices. Here. This. Me. Long-term, delayed gratification. These are also qualities that tend to encourage our sense of creative worth, helping us see who we are and what we do more holistically – as a journey.

Thoughts on perspective

This sense of *how* and *what* we value when it comes to creativity can seem a little detached from the day-to-day practice of making. However, the underlying position or perspective we adopt (consciously, or otherwise) will have a significant bearing on how far we can grow beyond our current abilities. We believe it's helpful to:

Begin with who *you* are, where *you* are from, your interests, strengths, weaknesses, experiences, etc. The things that set you apart from others. Your uniqueness. Your identity.

Value these qualities as *equal to*, albeit *different from*, the person next to you – rather than better or worse (dualism again). There is no competition.

Recognize that this distinctiveness can be harnessed as a powerful tool in your capacity to birth new ideas.

No one notices things the way you do. You are the only person who sees the world like you do, and that surely has to be celebrated if creativity is (as we believe), in part, an outward expression of the inner you, and which thrives when offered the chance to create new interpretations of old themes.

Focusing solely on the strength or weakness of the creative outcome ultimately emphasizes what any given novel, design or song can do for us. It reduces the value of creative work to a base product that is solely there for others to consume. It pays little or no respect to the benefits of creativity itself, let alone the person who made it, their uniqueness, and what the act of making did for them, or others. By focusing on your unique creativity as the thing of greatest value – rather than the outcomes you create – you can begin to redefine how you engage with new ideas, and develop a deep-rooted need to bring them to life.

You already have a manifesto

You and your work exist within a context that shapes and defines a *creative manifesto* – the how-you-do-whatever-it-is-you-already-do. By identifying your practice as a manifesto, you can start to reassess your sense of what constitutes success or failure, and address underlying creative problems along the way.

'Identifying how we go about doing anything is essential to modifying or gaining control over it.'

Neil Fiore [5]

Reflecting on and defining your existing practice in some detail is highly significant creatively, as experience suggests that these manifestos shape our growth in a variety of ways – some superficially, and (importantly) others far more deeply. Our manifestos – what we believe about ourselves and our craft – can simultaneously inhibit and enhance. Like driving a car with both the brake and accelerator engaged, we can expend significant energy trying to move but repeatedly find ourselves frustrated that we never seem to be getting very far. By identifying and giving language to both our historical and existing processes, we can pinpoint areas of strength and potential growth that are specific to us as individuals.

Our experience working with students has shown that the initial exploration to find the central focus, patterns and edges of your practice (the beginnings of your manifesto) can seem a little daunting, confusing or, occasionally, pointless. We all generally want a quick fix. The results, however, have proved pivotal in helping individuals move beyond their existing working habits, and experience a significant and positive shift in creative possibility. This book – and particularly the practice exercises in Chapter 4 – essentially constitute some of the attempts we've made to help with this process.

Know thy enemy

Much of this first chapter has been concerned with knowing yourself, or at least, offering some initial thoughts that begin to frame you and your current creative practice in a new light. In this penultimate part of the chapter we turn our attention to the dark side of creativity.

Sun Tzu was a Chinese military strategist, army general and philosopher from around the 6th century BC. His ideas found form in the seminal text *The Art of War* and his writings have influenced military strategy in both the East and West ever since. Steven Pressfield is an American writer with over a dozen novels to his name, including several bestsellers and a number that have been turned into films. His seminal text, *The War of Art*, is a nod to the strategies of Sun Tzu, but turns its gaze towards creativity rather than military might. Both reference the idea of knowing yourself and your enemy as a central component to the advancement of their respective battles.

'If you know the enemy and know yourself, you need not fear the result of a hundred battles. If you know yourself but not the enemy, for every victory gained you will also suffer a defeat. If you know neither the enemy nor yourself, you will succumb in every battle.'

Sun Tzu [6]

In *The War of Art*, Pressfield brilliantly and concisely personifies the idea of an opposing force (which he calls *resistance*) whose sole purpose is to distract, delay and, if possible, destroy the presence of any creative growth or productivity in your life. In our experience, *resistance* causes more creative impotence in students than we'd ever care to remember.

Self-doubt. Procrastination. Instant gratification and its capacity to render the need for any long-term effort entirely redundant. Comparison. The internal (or external) critic. Habit. Fear. Self-sabotage. You name it, they are all different facets of the same person.

You.
Know thy enemy.

At the end of the day, if you agree that creativity is something we are, rather than something we do, it follows that many of the problems with our creative growth are largely internal rather than external. We don't need to look far to find the root of the problem – and therein, lies the challenge. If our perspective is grounded in a belief that requires external affirmation (rather than accepting personal distinctiveness), encourages creative conformity (rather than embracing multiple processes), or is simply oblivious to the presence of any problem in the first place (what is your manifesto?), resistance has already won.

It happens to us all

The vital thing to recognize is that – as our own experiences thus far suggest – we all suffer from creative self-doubt. We all procrastinate. We are all guilty of self-sabotage. No one is immune, and there even seems to be a direct correlation between a growing awareness of our creative potential ('I can do this', 'This has value', 'I'm improving'...) and our increasing fears that it may all crash and burn around us. Even veterans of the creative world carry the burden of resistance – the difference is how they respond to the pressure. Knowing that none of us are immune is a vital first step. Knowing that we can use negatives to our advantage

'The enemy is Resistance.'

Steven Pressfield [7]

is the beginning of real creative maturity. Neil Fiore again: 'Once we've identified specific negative behaviours, we can actually use their onset to rechannel our behaviour in a more desirable direction.'[8]

The thing we have in common

The central tenet of this book is to position you, the individual, at the heart of the equation. Almost everything we've written tries to avoid generic assumptions; we've attempted to frame each example or exercise in the light of a unique creative process: yours! That said, there's one recurring behaviour that we have seen in (nearly) all of our students, so let's pause here and address it before we move on.

Conversations containing the word *edit* are, without a doubt, THE most common form of guidance we've given in over 30 years of collective teaching. And, if there was one, deliberate alteration you could make to your practice that would produce an immediate and dramatic change, considering how you currently edit could well be it. Editing is arguably the single most critical skill you can develop to enhance your creativity – particularly when trying to come up with new ideas.

Or, to be more specific, knowing when or when not to edit is the single most important skill you can develop to enhance your creativity. The challenge is knowing what state to be in, and at what point in your process to be in it.

Freefall

Generally, when we consciously develop ideas, we simultaneously make value judgements on them. These are often along the lines of 'Is it any good?', 'Will it work?', 'Does it solve the problem?', 'Is it original?', 'Will they (whoever they are) like it?', 'Can I practically produce it?' And so on. These judgements are lightning quick and rapid in succession, so we tend to go with what appears to be instinct. As ideas appear, we eliminate or edit them out: 'It doesn't feel right', 'I can't see how it will work', 'It's been done before', 'I don't know how to make it'. We often tend to reject creative thoughts straight away because we can't yet see the idea in finished form. It's this impulsive, external dismissal of what is also the less-immediate internal potential in every idea that we are trying to protect.

Our identity shapes an expansive, one-of-a-kind view of the world that we need to protect, celebrate and nurture.

'Students are not privy to the process behind the work they admire. They see the final form, a wonderful Golden Sphere... What they may not understand is that this sphere is made out of little bits, small discoveries, pieces carefully fitted together, plastered over, sanded, refashioned, painted, lacquered and then finally given the golden coating. It looks like it sprung full blown out of someone's head, when in fact it was the result of hard work and an uncertain process.'

Saul Bass [9]

The (mistaken) assumption is that every idea needs to be fully formed at the point of conception. We edit out anything that does not fit a very limiting set of conditions (often based on known or safe qualities that have worked in the past – see Chapter 2), and in doing so, reduce the creative pool of possibility significantly. However, most great ideas tend to reveal themselves over time, often resulting from an iterative, subconscious process that chips, shapes and refines early (and possibly risky) ideas through to their fully formed state.

New ideas are the result of a variety of elements mixing, jarring and fusing, and it takes a lifetime of practice to refine this process. It's almost as if those elements – the building blocks of ideas, such as people, place, context, technology, language, image, text, message – have a life of their own, each needing to become an active part of an evolving recipe. We must give initial ideas the space to move and grow beyond their original form, thereby nurturing their potential. We need to embrace a period of creative freefall, allowing ideas to simply flow – irrespective of where we might be heading, or what our initial assumptions may be. Henry Moore said it this way: 'If I set out to sculpt a standing man and it becomes a lying woman, I know I am making art...'[10] Good ideas need time to mature, to respond to the contextual factors that shape culture. Every block of stone has a statue inside it and it is the task of the sculptor to discover it.[11] You can replace 'block of stone' with any working material, and 'sculptor' with any working practice; the principle is the same. Nurturing anything involves discovery and dialogue – back and forth, responding and adapting, being open to possibility, and adopting an approach that does not rule anything out (or *edit*), at least initially.

Any noticeable editing during this early idea development can stunt growth or limit creative potential, and this seems to get worse the older we get. Kids have an amazing ability to imagine and play, simply because they haven't yet learnt that editing is even necessary ('Every child is an artist. The problem is how to remain an artist once we grow up' – Pablo Picasso[12]). Switching off (or dulling) the editing part of our thinking – at least temporarily – to allow creative flow has exciting implications both in the short-term development of a specific idea, but also in the long-term exercising of our 'curiosity muscle'.[13]

Balance

There is, of course, a real danger that spending too much time in a state of non-editing freefall will result in an overwhelming number of possibilities. A new problem then arises – one of conceptual glut. This can grow to the point where you no longer see the wood for the trees; you forget what you were looking for in the first place, and you end up going round in circles. Kids are great at play, but ask them to tidy up, stop or do anything that demands they come out of their creative world and they're likely to object. In our design experience, and our observations of students' development, this excess of possibilities, and the subsequent inability to move forward, is fairly common. Learning when to edit, therefore, is vital. And even when the time is right, the editing in itself is a skill that can take years to refine. When you are aware of both states, the flow/edit balance gradually comes into its own.

Allowing yourself a greater degree of freedom to simply let ideas emerge (by including every initial thought, and not editing anything out) means that when you subsequently choose to edit, you're selecting the better ideas from the bunch. You're also likely to see more connections between some of the less obvious starting points, and get as many usable ideas by combining several less-viable sparks, as you will viable ideas straight off the bat. Overall, the total number of ideas increases

significantly when editing occurs after, rather than during, a period of creative freefall. In our teaching experience, this has proved to be almost universally the case.

Compare this to what is often our default process of editing as we go. We end up with fewer recorded thoughts (because we fail to give potential ideas the chance to fly), which in turn gives us less to work with, which means fewer connections, and ultimately fewer usable ideas at the end of the day. Habit and the need for an immediate fix trick us into moving on too soon, and we miss out on the richness that lies just beneath the surface. It's a no-brainer, and yet we all fall into the edit trap. Resisting the urge to edit is a discipline that must be developed and then maintained, whatever your age or experience. We've included several practical exercises in Chapter 4 that address some of this thinking more directly.

As an afterthought, you will likely know people who describe themselves as 'not creative'. Does this have more to do with their edit switch being permanently on, or a default belief that their ideas are no good? Or unoriginal? Or impractical? Or don't feel right? Are there individuals who reject their ideas so quickly, harshly and regularly that, over time, their process has effectively shut down their creative expression altogether? Perhaps saying 'I'm not creative' is just easier than embracing temporary failure in the service of longer-term success.

~~Edit.~~ What if...?
Edit. ~~What if...?~~
Repeat.

Summary

We are all unique, and this uniqueness is, we believe, fundamental to understanding how we think about creativity. Our identity shapes an expansive, one-of-a-kind view of the world that we need to protect, celebrate and nurture. By extension, there are processes – multiple ways of engaging in creative practice – and the journey to discover what works for you is as important as the work you create, if not more so.

Beyond this, the qualities that define your existing practice – your manifesto – are your creative ground. This is the foundation that you build upon, so understanding its strengths (and weaknesses) is vital to the longevity of your craft. And central to this self-reflection is acknowledging that there's always resistance to our creative growth. However, understanding our enemy (our self) is integral to moving forward, and often the liberating act that leads to significant positive change.

Finally, a reminder that this entire book is centred around you as an individual, and your creative process. That said, positive development is also rooted in being open to learning from others, adopting an attitude that seeks out opportunity, and accepts that we're all still growing. The need for balance is vital – and our collective tendency to edit out potential ideas too early is just one example of this. We'll address an understanding of these habits in Chapter 2, then go on to look at how play (Chapter 3) can serve as a simple antidote to even the most challenging creative blocks. Practice (Chapter 4) then rolls the whole story together into a series of hands-on exercises that address the themes of identity, habit and play, in a wide variety of ways.

We're just warming up...

Chapter 2

Habit

Chapter 2:

Habit

'In order to be creative, you have to know how to prepare to be creative.'

Twyla Tharp [1]

Introduction

We believe too much in creativity not to suppose that there are a multitude of creative methods, models or ways of operating as a creative person. Too often, in the conversations surrounding the subject, we're told what to do, how to behave, what the convention is or what a particular 'magic formula' might be. The commodification of creative thinking through attempts to package and market a repeatable formula (that often promises to guarantee success) compromises creativity in a way that misses a fundamental point: there is no *one* true creative process. As the proverbial saying goes, there are many ways to skin a cat (although we don't encourage felicide in any way!).

To better prepare ourselves to be creative, we believe it's essential to be mindful of the social structures and mechanisms that frame *how* people create. It's vital to first view the patterns, constraints or routines we (and others) apply to our own practice. Only then are we able to make up our minds and consciously choose our own way of operating.

Models for harnessing our creativity are great. There are many examples provided in this book (mainly in Chapter 4), and plenty more elsewhere. There is, however, a key underlying principle we have learnt from observing and utilizing them that's central to achieving any long-term growth – namely:

We are creatures of habit. Habits are hard to form, and they are even harder to break.

All the evidence suggests that adopting good working habits is hard – the sheer volume of people who join a gym in January only to leave it before March is testament to this. But what's the use in us sharing various creativity-improving methodologies if we all find them hard to adopt? We need to understand the mechanics of habit better.

We form habits after learning something new. Charles Duhigg, the author of *The Power of Habit*, refers to this as a three-step process known as a *habit loop*.[2] First, there's a cue, a trigger that tells your brain to go into automatic mode and prompts which habit to use. Then there's the routine, which can be physical, mental or emotional. Finally, there's a reward, which helps your brain figure out if this particular loop is worth remembering for the future.

For example: cue = alarm clock >> routine = go for a run >> reward = feel great >> repeat.

Or the reality version: cue = alarm clock >> routine = have a lie-in >> reward = feel great >> repeat.

Having insight and applying it are two different things and, all too often with this subject, there is not enough focus on the latter. Unless acted upon, meaningful insights around systems and processes are, quite simply, useless.

So, how can we adopt better working methods? One answer lies in the notion of acting contrary to our existing habits. Anything that stops us doing what we'd normally do will elicit a response that facilitates creativity in some way. Remember (and please excuse this oversimplification), *we normally do what we normally do*, and any disruption to that *normal* system will force us to do something *we don't normally do*. This is important for many reasons (which we'll describe later), but mainly because it adds novelty and creates a puzzle to solve – both of which invoke curiosity, which is a fundamental driver of creativity. Our brain seeks the comfort of its typical pattern and strives to find it. Yet, as the starting point is in

wilko

Falmouth
TR11 3AS - 01326210359
VAT: GB125596651 www.wilko.com

Nail Clipper
Coaster
Airer
Airer

TOTAL [3]
card

CUSTOMER RECEIPT

£P7.00
£P7.00

CONTACTLESS
PLEASE KEEP THIS RECEIPT FOR YOUR
RECORDS
AUTH CODE:076666

	VAT	GROSS	NET
A 20%	£1.17	£7.00	£5.83

You were served by: Self

30/09/20 16:08 000408 0105 0041 99999905

****
Share how you feel about your experience
at www.yourwinningthoughts.com
for a chance
to win a £100 Wilko Gift Card
****

0010408300920105000041

This page: Algorithm—Freedom, collage by Abbie Macphail (see page 214 Combine)

unfamiliar territory, its journey back to the safety of the known inevitably covers new ground.

Our natural reaction to any given situation tends to be habitual, and our creativity is similarly rooted in learnt habits; we are just not always aware of it. By identifying and understanding our habits and tendencies, we can better understand how we might make positive changes to any ingrained habit loops when it comes to working creatively.

The limitations of habit

The word *process* suggests a sequence or a series of actions taking place; incremental change and connections being made. With most individual creative processes, we tend to repeat specific actions. This repetition is important in any creative process, as it helps us improve and gives us confidence that we can achieve positive results.

When someone is stuck or suffering from a creative block, more often than not it's due to them being locked into a particular point of view or way of approaching the task in hand. An overly familiar process, with patterns of behaviour embedded as routine, can become the very thing that prevents us from getting unstuck. The definition of progress is to break old patterns in order to advance.

Habits, in and of themselves, are not inherently good or bad – they're clearly important in the gaining of skills and expertise. Indeed, becoming an expert at something, or being a professional, means that we have learnt, through repetition, how to do something well, and we have affirmed what we know. However, in the case of creativity, this acquired knowledge can also mean experimentation or creative risks are avoided as the path is too firmly laid down. By accepting our specialist status and all its implicit restrictions, open-mindedness is often neglected.

The way we respond to any particular problem is based on our collected and stored frames of reference. If you have ever burnt your hand in a fire, on seeing fire again, the memory of that previous experience will prevent you from repeating the action.

'The most fundamental cause of artist's block is connected to the inability to simply let go of premeditation.'

Shaun McNiff [3]

Our creativity works in the same way. When confronted with a specific problem, we develop a tendency to respond in a particular way. Once our response has been laid down several times, it becomes a pathway.

You may have noticed the occasional dirt pathway cutting through a section of grass in a park, providing a shortcut away from the paved path. This *desire line*, as it's known, shows a potential fault in the design of the original path, not fully considering the path of least resistance someone may wish to take (especially if they're in a hurry). Once enough people have followed this shorter route, the dirt path becomes wider, and the grass isn't given a chance to grow back. Taking the easy route may get us there faster, but it may not always be the right choice, especially if it limits our experience (or damages the lawn in the process).

Desire lines serve as a useful analogy to the creative process and the limitations of habit. If we think of the creative process as a pathway, when we react to any given situation, we will more often than not take the path that's known to us. Much of the inspiration for this book (and most of Chapter 4) has been an attempt to document possible new paths one could take in the pursuit of a creative solution, and that chapter touches more on the subject of desire lines. If we act contrary to habit in the context of generating new ideas, we're not only attempting to think and respond in a new way, we're also adding new frames of reference to our memory (which we may recall at a later date). Even if the specific idea created in this way is not the most suitable, the new process itself acts as a form of idea-generation training and provides fuel for future creative

'Plato used the expression *techne tou biou*, which means "the craft of life." When *techne* is defined with sufficient depth, it refers not just to mechanical skills and instruments but to all kinds of artful managing and careful shaping ... we can say that care of the soul requires a special crafting of life itself, with an artist's sensitivity to the way things are done. Soul doesn't pour into life automatically. It requires our skill and attention.'

Thomas Moore [4]

Think of yourself as having a dual personality. One side of this personality is emotional, playful, biased (the artist). The other is organized, practical and considered (the guardian).

challenges. In this way, we believe that new experiences are the raw material for creativity.

Routines (life)

When we consider our creative tendencies, we find many parallels in our daily lives. After all, who we are is the precursor to how we operate.

If we build on the Greek concept of *techne tou biou* and imagine the design of our daily routines and working practices as an artwork in its own right, what opportunities might this provide for framing our own creative experiences? Yes, the novelty of it may make our lives more interesting (and surely it's worth the effort for this alone), but will it make us more creative? A colleague of ours, Lizzie Ridout, often encourages students to 'treat everything you do like an artwork', whether it's sending an email, leaving a thank you note or baking a cake. Every activity holds within it a creative opportunity and an aesthetic meaning. If this truly is the case, then spending time crafting our simple daily routines is undoubtedly worthy of our attention.

'What I've found with daily routines, is that the useful thing is to have one that feels new. It can almost be arbitrary. You know, you could say to yourself, "from now on, I'm only going to write on the back porch in flip flops starting at four o'clock in the afternoon." And if it feels novel and fresh, it will have a placebo effect and it will help you work.'

Nicholson Baker [5]

For many of us, these new routines can be quite simple; their benefit is more to do with the repetition and discipline of a set timetable to live by than with anything particularly innovative about the actions involved. Creating a set routine can be a survival technique for many people – without setting the right conditions, creativity can become too much of a struggle. It's this regime of discipline that sets the stage for the arrival of creativity. Order leads to action. Structure leads to chance.

The novelty aspect of a new routine or way of working shouldn't be dismissed; the line between novelty and innovation can be a thin one. New perspectives are the life blood of creativity, so exposure to new experiences is an essential raw material if our creative work is to evolve.

Time

The theories of routine, habit and order are all ultimately concerned with one thing: how we organize our time. As stated previously, a process suggests a series of actions taking place, so considering which steps to take, when to take them, and how long to spend doing so is of utmost importance. Designing a routine means organizing our time, the most valuable and perhaps limited resource we have.

When it comes to the cyclical nature of research and idea generation, the most common barrier to progress is a type of procrastination. Knowing when to move on to the next stage, to actually realize our emerging ideas and bring something to life is one of the most common stumbling blocks. Students often believe that the best idea is just around the corner, when it might actually be something already down on the page. The temptation to explore continuously is more often than not a delaying technique, a clever avoidance habit that distances us from the need to make a decision. We simultaneously convince ourselves that we are productive, which further compounds the problem, and this lingering doubt prevents us from making positive choices.

How, then, can we make an informed decision in moments like these? How do we know when to take action, or when to stop, so that we can move on? Earlier in this chapter, we chastised those who talk of creative magic formulas – snake-oil salesmen who have a simple answer to our problems. However, when it comes to the problem of not knowing when to make the best choice, it turns out we can turn to the world of mathematics for one possible answer. The principle lies in something called the *optimal stopping theory*, and the answer is 37 per cent. Now, this does feel a bit like the answer to the meaning of life (42) in *The Hitchhiker's Guide to the Galaxy*. A little bit disappointing and meaningless, but hear us out...

In *Algorithms to Live By* by Brian Christian and Tom Griffiths, the theory of optimal stopping is described as being 'concerned with the problem of choosing a time to take a given action.'[6] After looking at several options to choose from (be it ideas, houses or partners), the best odds on securing the top option of all those we will see will occur after we've seen 37 per cent of them (or spent 37 per cent of the time we have available to look). This look-then-leap rule suggests a way of combating the debilitating moment we often find ourselves in when we don't know when to commit to making a choice. When we apply this rule to the selection of an idea, it will look as follows: Define how much time we have, and spend the first 37 per cent of this time creating ideas. Then (statistically speaking), should we choose our current best idea at this point, we are likely to have selected the best idea we were ever likely to generate.

It's important to note at this point that *measuring* creativity is not something we're interested in at all. The obsession with measurement is education's biggest problem and is a direct contributor to the significant rise in mental-health issues across all levels of education and beyond. So, we need to be careful not to hold ourselves to account with the numbers. Highlighting this theory is simply one definite way of reducing the anxiety of choice – just spend roughly a third of our time not choosing, then choose the best we have available to us. It's not foolproof, but in many cases *done* is better than *perfect,* and if, like us, you are not as prolific as you'd dearly like to be, then try applying the 37 per cent rule to your creative process and see what happens.

Knowing when to stop is also important in relation to our work ethic. The tendency is to believe that those who work the longest hours produce the best results. Hard work should be a given (in work and university alike) but not at the expense of our quality of life or the quality of our creative output. We're led to believe that opportunities are everywhere for the hard-workers and grafters, strivers, opportunists and can-doers – after all, we live in the age of the entrepreneur. This prevailing attitude, combined with the precarious nature of work is, we believe, an enemy of creativity. The culture of the *entreprecariat*[7] is both unhelpful and unhealthy – for us and for our creativity. And it can also be argued that it is inefficient.

We certainly believe in the virtue of hard work, but not in wasted effort. The current culture of 'smashing it' seems to harm people's wellbeing; this must be replaced by an ethos that's more nurturing and supportive. By focusing our attention on crafting our daily routines and rituals, we can better nourish our creative minds, while also taking into consideration (much more holistically) the impact on our physical and mental health.

Movement

Often in our creative process, we get stuck in a rut, and our thoughts can feel like they're moving incredibly slowly – or sometimes not at all. This is a normal and regular occurrence for most of us. Our brains get tired, primarily as a result of either working for too long, or working on the same task without any real sense of progress. Much like reviewing our use of time (and the tendency to over-exert ourselves), considering the relationship between mental and physical fatigue – and particularly, how we use the space around us, and our movement in and around that space – can also work incredibly well.

It could be as simple as moving from one room to another. It's not that your other room contains a fresh burst of mental energy (although we're sure it's a lovely space) – it is more likely that the simple act of walking itself is the thing that helps us. It's scientifically proven that a brisk walk increases not just our physical and mental wellbeing but also our creative capabilities, so planning such activities into our day should become a regular and deliberate practice. We believe that movement is integral to any creative practice and, as university lecturers, there is no sight more depressing than a student chained to their desk for an entire day. Such prolonged presence in one spot – like a time-lapse film, with the business of the world moving all around them – may well demonstrate a commendable work ethic, and arguably, a real feat of endurance, yet it's unlikely to be as creative, productive or healthy as they believe it to be.

The artist and the guardian

At this point, it would be helpful to present a working metaphor that we know has helped us understand creativity better than anything else, that of the *artist* and the *guardian*. Think of yourself as having a dual personality. One side of this personality is emotional, playful, biased (the artist). The other is organized, practical and considered (the guardian).

This page: Artist—Guardian, collage by Hannah De Oliveira Whitlock (see page 214 Combine)

We all have both, although the proportions will vary from person to person, and even from project to project. The artist is the creative personality and is highly sensitive, so one of the guardian's key roles is to keep the artist at arm's length from any criticism that may interfere with its natural creativity. We already know that our minds operate on these two levels simultaneously: the artist, unconscious and self-activating, and the guardian, conscious and appraising.

These two working systems were notably described by Daniel Kahneman as *System 1* and *System 2*.[8] In various other scientific texts they've been described as *hot* and *cool*, *heuristic processing* and *analytical processing*, and even simply *automatic* and *reflective*. Much has been written about the role of the limbic (emotional) and the neocortex (logical) segments of our brain, and their roles in terms of decision-making. In her book *Becoming a Writer*, Dorothea Brande talked of the importance of understanding the *unconscious* and the *conscious*.[9] John Cleese (of Monty Python fame) referred to being in one of two modes (*open* and *closed*).[10] The literature on the subject of creativity is littered with such dichotomies. Even the glib maxim often misattributed to Ernest Hemingway,[11] 'write drunk, edit sober', fits perfectly with the notion of the artist and the guardian, metaphorically at least, although for health and safety reasons we are certainly *not* encouraging you to reach for the bottle! Whichever of these analogous juxtapositions you prefer, they all illustrate the same position: the tension between *that which we can control* and *that which we cannot*.

Ideas are simply a new combination of known elements, and they are the result of unconscious recombination (by our artist selves).[12] Nietzsche noted that 'A thought comes when it wills, not when I will it.'[13] Often, the error in our collective understanding of any creative process (in higher education and in industry) is assuming a relationship between cause and effect – do *this*, and *that* will happen. It may do, yet it may not. We can provide the conditions for connections to occur, but that connection cannot be forced. You can lead a horse to water, but you may not be able to make it understand Nietzsche's critique of phenomenology as a reliable guide to causation. (We think Dion may have written that joke while in Hemingway's drunk mode.)

So, we know we cannot control creativity; all we can do is try to harness it. And this is where the guardian can come in, by reconfiguring and presenting new information to the artist in a way that may allow new combinations to occur.

Provocation

What happens to our existing habit loops when our guardian deliberately behaves in a more provocative way – not in an attempt to organize our thinking, but to explore ways in which to disorganize it?

For the past few years, we've been exploring this question of disruptive processes in several ways, most notably in the form of our Warrior Mode workshops (see pp. 98–105), wherein we get students to create the antithesis of their usual working process and then ask them to use it faithfully for a small project. We encourage students to deliberately act contrary to habit (often quite exceptionally so). The results? Well, you'd expect them all to fail in quite spectacular fashion. And in one sense, they do (the exercise is specifically designed as such). Actively choosing to ignore the point of a brief, or going to sleep for the day, or doing no initial research all tend to have a negative effect on your average student project. However, in a surprising number of cases, the Warrior Modes don't fail at all. Each time we've run these workshops, many students have found that their new working method has allowed them to create something unexpectedly positive, or has highlighted an approach that's offered the basis of a new working habit. What this approach does best is to enable them to identify flaws in their current working practice, as well as affirm what's already working well. When they return to their habitual way of working, they'll often make minor (or, occasionally major) adjustments in order to refine their practice, adopting deliberate 'failure' mechanisms in the early stages of a given project to broaden their creative reach.

Failure and creativity are intrinsically linked, and therein lies our problem with measuring creativity (and assessment in particular). Education is built on the premise of getting it right from an early age, subsequently branding failure as a negative and therefore as something to be avoided at all costs. By consciously setting ourselves up to fail from the outset (as a deliberate and controlled process – overseen by our guardian), our artist is far more likely to embrace non-familiar habits, explore uncharted territory, and discover new ideas and concepts.

When we work without boundaries, we more often than not drown in a sea of possibility.

Our ongoing creation of workshops of this kind – and, indeed, the primary motivation for writing this book – is based on the realization that through a process of *discovery learning*, we can encourage as many students as possible to shift their perspectives again and again, until they become comfortable with this dislocation. Through these experiences, they naturally identify and adopt their points of reference, ultimately developing the tools, processes and routines that reflect their unique creative personalities. Identity and habit come (almost) full circle.

Creative constraints: the guardian as algorithm

Finally, then, to the idea of creative constraints. When we work without boundaries, we more often than not drown in a sea of possibility. Unabridged freedom may, on the surface, appear to be the ultimate goal – you can do *whatever you like*. However, there is arguably nothing more suffocating for creativity, and we often end up fearing the open brief. Constraints provide us with a safe space, a protected context to operate within, and afford us one less thing to think about.

Constraints are used as a means of triggering ideas and inspiration, and many lateral-thinking tests provide specific limitations for us to work within. Sometimes the presentation of the constraints themselves is just as compelling as the response. For example, OuLiPo (Ouvroir de littérature potentielle, which roughly translates as 'workshop of potential literature') is a collection of mainly Francophone writers and mathematicians who impose constrained writing techniques upon themselves in pursuit of creativity. It was founded in 1960 by Raymond Queneau and François Le Lionnais. Notable works generated by OuLiPo members include Queneau's *Cent mille milliards de poèmes*, a collection of ten sonnets that could be recombined in a hundred thousand billion different ways (and would probably take 200 million years to read), and Georges Perec's novel *La Disparition*, which does not contain the letter *e*. The movement has also inspired other non-writing groups, such as OuBaPo (Ouvroir de bande dessinée potentielle, established in 1992), members of which create comic book art under voluntary artistic constraints in a similar way.

Queneau defined the purpose of OuLiPo as 'the search for new forms and structures that may be used by writers in any way they see fit.'[14]

Choosing a formal constraint from the outset (write a novel without using the letter e, design a website without using a computer, draw a still life while blindfolded) allows us to focus on a specific problem, rather than becoming lost in the expansive nature of an open brief. It also offers the satisfaction of a successful outcome – if the novel we write contains no e's, then congratulations, it's a success! Our mind is distracted from self-doubt or an analysis of the merits of the content because it's busy essentially solving a puzzle. You can see the parallels here with our earlier thoughts (Chapter 1) on the traditional metrics governing creative success (book deals, design awards, record contracts), and their limiting potential on our creative expression. In our attempts to create the perfect puzzle analogy to summarize these thoughts, we discovered that Queneau had beaten us to it, describing OuLiPoans as 'rats who build the labyrinth from which they will try to escape.'[15] When we use constraints as a conceptual framework (or, to describe in another way – when the guardian thinks like an artist), it can minimize the labour of thought and be incredibly freeing. Indeed, constraints = freedom.

Summary

Creative work results from the combination of ideas and craft – the will of meaning towards form. If we propose a puzzle to solve (in bringing form to our ideas), the focus is on the process itself and the joy of figuring it out, rather than how it's ultimately achieved. Often, the more difficult the puzzle, the better it feels to finally solve it. Or, as Queneau said, 'the more intricate the labyrinth, the happier the rat who escapes from it.'[16]

Writing briefs for ourselves, applying formal constraints to our approach, systematically challenging, changing and reordering our daily routines and rituals are all attempts to create the perfect labyrinth from which we will escape.

All good so far. Next, a look at how play can serve as a simple antidote to even the most challenging creative blocks.

Opposite: Craft—Life, collage by Millie Burdon (see page 214 Combine)

Play

Chapter 3:

Play

'Life must be
lived as play...'

Plato [1]

Introduction

Play: a mood, behaviour or performance. It can be fun, rewarding, positive, spontaneous, exaggerated or competitive. It can happen in a safe place, on a sports field or a stage.

This chapter is about understanding the role of play and playfulness in enabling creativity. Play has multiple meanings, depending on the context used, and it's often regarded as an activity for the young. In children, play is often a form of training or preparation for dealing with adulthood, which is why on reaching adulthood, we tend to play less. However, play can also be incredibly useful as a generator of new thoughts, ideas and behaviours.

When children play, they create a prototype of the world around them, stepping inside and immersing themselves in it. When we are playing, we loosen our hold on what we know to be true – we imagine that which is not (which sounds very much like a description for being creative). So, it stands to reason that play can be a crucial driver of creativity.

In our years of teaching design and creative thinking, we have overheard many tutors saying to students (and we're complicit in this): 'Just go and play with that idea for a while' – or words to that effect. What's being offered here is a positive encouragement to loosen up and become more experimental with the work. We've noticed, however, that this invitation to play doesn't always translate for the student. You could argue that it's ambiguous. 'Do they mean, adopt a playful attitude?', 'Should I physically play with it like a cat with a ball of string?', 'Are they using the word *play* as a verb?', 'Should I play it like a game?' And so on.

When we consider the overwhelming array of individual actions someone might take in response to this instruction, there's clearly a need to be more specific. It's part of human nature to want to play, but once we have become boring grown-ups with responsibilities, we may well have forgotten how to harness the power of play. This third chapter therefore offers some concrete suggestions for how we might 'play with that idea', and how we can adopt a more playful approach to solving a specific problem.

Activity and exploration

Much of what happens in education is set up to focus on facts and serious work and outcomes in an environment where everything you do is measured and assessed. This seems counterproductive when we know that play (and education) is most rewarding when the players (and students) are protected from the consequences of their creative (or academic) behaviour.

Decades of research on creativity has taught us that playfulness, creative risk and innovation all work best in an environment where quantifiable measurement is absent, yet sadly, this knowledge isn't utilized by most schools or universities. This, together with our bias towards teaching students to remember facts in order to recall them during an exam, is crippling any sense of adaptability, and fostering an inability to deal with uncertainty (another critical facet of creativity).

Numerous experiments by the psychologist Teresa Amabile have revealed that any intervention which increases the *incentive* to be creative (prizes or rewards, and, by extension, academic grades) has the effect of reducing creativity.[2] In experiment after experiment, participants who were under the impression that their outcomes would not be evaluated (so, no prizes, rewards or grades) – essentially thinking they were just creating for fun – were more likely to produce the most

Opposite:
Fun—Serious, collage by Chris Ireland (see page 214 Combine)

creative outcomes. So, it seems that being in a *non-incentive* condition (playing) is essential when it comes to creativity.

Learning, creativity and problem-solving are all improved by anything that will promote a state of playfulness. Conversely, learning, creativity and problem-solving are all significantly inhibited by things that interfere with playfulness, such as evaluation or an expectation of rewards. In most contexts, the pressure of assessment and measurement will impair someone's performance. The only caveat to this is when we've already achieved a high skill level at a particular task, in which case the pressure of measurement may not always have a detrimental effect. Students who are *just playing* at something tend to do better than those who are trying to impress an assessor, unless they are highly skilled and practised.

If someone wants to increase the amount of manual labour we do, then sure, they can incentivize us by paying us £100 an hour, and we'll be likely to work harder, faster and better. Dangling carrots can improve our performance of those tasks. But the same is not the case with creativity. Quite simply, you cannot be more creative just by trying harder.

Creativity happens under a particular set of conditions, and is more difficult to achieve in the presence of incentives. Peter Gray summarizes this in his book *Free to Learn*: 'The pressure to perform well interferes with new learning and pressure to be creative interferes with creativity.'[3]

Freud's thinking on human behaviour and play suggests that there's a balance between understanding our wishes and the role of play in seeing them realized. Humans need to be active and to explore. If we are missing either of these things in our life, it can drive us nuts and be bad for our health. We are complex and dynamic creatures, and to us, monotony is intolerable. Play is central.

Activity (any specific action or pursuit)

We can talk about play as an attitude in terms of how we might approach an activity. Consider play as the mood of the person rather than what they are doing. What is an indicator of being in a playful mood? How might we signal it? We laugh. And when we laugh, we throw off restraint. In a relaxed mood, we're encouraged to take creative risks and try new things. We also enjoy it more because, through play, an activity becomes pleasurable. For example, we play the piano (and enjoy it). We do not play an Excel spreadsheet (or enjoy it).

Exploration (to examine or investigate)

Play, like research, is a form of exploration, but play is less cautious and intense due to generally not having any immediate practical goals. A playful state of mind is harder to achieve if we focus too hard on the facts. If everything is *known* then there are fewer opportunities to speculate on how things *could be*. Almost by definition,

'...[a sole] focus on "knowledge" (that which is already known) seems in opposition to our society's belief in creativity as the act of bringing forth something new. On the other hand, knowledge of what has been, and is, generally functions as a prerequisite to creating anything that has not yet been...'

Paul Weiner [4]

So, how can we become more playful? Is it something we turn on like a switch (especially if being playful isn't our natural state of being)? Most of us, in our adult lives, are performing the responsible roles expected of us, and they often inhibit us. Indeed, a good way of seeing these formal inhibitions in action is to watch how people behave around small children. Which of us are prepared to play along with a child's game? Some individuals don't ever step up to engage. Children are a no-go area – too far out of the established comfort zone. Some take a while to loosen up, initially reluctant to join a child at an imaginary tea-party, for example. Others immediately regress to a child-like state and are then overwhelmingly welcomed into the fun. Anxieties around how our performance might be perceived by others (even small children) can be a restricting barrier to being playful. The same is true in our creative practice. Worrying about what others will think prevents many of us from enjoying the process of creativity or the notion of playing within our work, and it's a concern we have seen increase among our students in recent

All creative outputs are the results of our pretending, whether it's a film, stage play, painting or logo. It's all simply manipulated fiction. If we accept in advance that our outcomes are fiction, then it can release some of the tensions many of us have around behaving in unconventional ways.

years – the curse of oversensitive empathy. Still, perhaps it's better than not caring at all.

Being creatively oversensitive or worrying about how others will respond is a natural part of any creative process (the artist at work). There is, we believe, a clue to addressing these inhibitions located within the heart of play itself – the idea of pretending. As the adage goes, *you have to fake it till you make it*. When a small child asks you to become a bionic horse-monster, you just have to pretend you're a bionic horse-monster (and maybe initially just pretend to enjoy it)!

Make-believe play is central to all creative disciplines. We (designers, writers, artists, illustrators, filmmakers, and so on) are the creators of fiction. We bring to life things that previously did not exist. When we ask 'What if?' and give form to our answers, we're essentially just pretending. All creative outputs are the results of our pretending, whether it's a film, stage play, painting or logo. It's all simply manipulated fiction. If we accept in advance that our outcomes are fiction, then it can release some of the tensions many of us have around behaving in unconventional ways. Through this pretence, we open ourselves up to being more optimistic, which in turn prevents us from shutting ideas down too early for not being realistic. We have seen countless students take significant shifts in their productivity by simply redefining what they do day to day as *design fiction*. It grants them a licence to play. And play is the game-changer.

Play does require immersion in an *otherness* – something sufficiently different from our ordinary reality. If an activity is too real, it's not play, and if it doesn't feel like play, we never cross the line into make-believe. We regularly seek this otherness when we read books, watch films or play video games, and can immerse ourselves almost entirely in these fictional worlds. We should try to seek this otherness in our practice, too. (A number of the exercises in Chapter 4 encourage this, including 'Warrior Mode' on pp. 98–105, 'Library Book Persona' on pp. 106–111, and 'Child's Play' on pp. 184–187). Play. Make-believe. Pretend. Be naïve and optimistic. Be a bionic horse-monster if you have to. See what happens.

What are you playing for?

Finally, it's important to remember that we can spend much of our creativity engaging with someone else's agenda or working to solve a specific problem, especially when working commercially. This makes it difficult to suspend our judgement or to ignore any potential end-product in the pursuit of a playful approach, but we do believe it's possible. If our goal is clear (and having a clear goal is generally a good idea), we can try not to focus on it too directly – averting our gaze for a time, holding it in the corner of our eye and only referencing the goal once in a while. We temporarily *devalue* the goal, loosening our grip on the centre to see what changes around the edges. The term *limited sloppiness,* which was coined by Max Delbrück, is useful here: 'Be sloppy enough so that something unexpected happens, but not so sloppy that you can't tell what it is.'[5] Forgetting or deliberately ignoring our objective for a defined period is one way of averting our gaze. Another way is to rephrase our brief again and again so that it begins to lose some of its meaning, or it shifts in focus, then periodically check back in with your original objective. This is different from altering the brief (which can be dangerous), as it still honours the prime focus, but acknowledges that a change of perspective can help nurture creative ideas. It may also feel like our artist and guardian are playing a game of hide and seek, and this is certainly not an easy thing to do – especially if we've passed through an education system that places great emphasis on intense concentration. However, by relaxing our focus, we provide the opportunity for new and creative things to happen and, as with most things, practice makes us better.

Hide and seek? Limited sloppiness? This is all beginning to sound like fun. Well, it should be. Creativity, or the generation of novelty, should be fun, right?

Right.
And wrong.
Wait. What?

It is important to have fun (as this creates the atmosphere needed for creativity to happen) but not too much fun; hyper-excitable positive mood states are not conducive to creativity.[6] Just as being too serious can negatively affect our creativity, so too can having too much fun. It seems, much like anything in life, it's all about finding a healthy balance. Sadly, we don't think we can provide you with a specific answer regarding the optimum balance – in part, due to us all responding and engaging with play in very different ways (optimal stopping theory doesn't work here). That said, our experiences suggest that by looping between a state of *play* to a state of *serious focus* – like moving from a bouncy castle to a writing desk – we will notice something of value along the way that will work for us.

The practice of improvisation

'When the one economic constant, ironically, is instability; when all aspects of our lives are driven by exponentially quickening technological change; and when education is increasingly under pressure to train people for jobs that by the time of their graduation are often no longer needed, it is increasingly the case that the best performances – human, corporate, or technological – are improvisational.'

Ric Knowles [7]

We live in fast-changing times. Everything seems to be in a constant state of flux. The only thing not changing is people saying 'we live in fast-changing times'. An ability to improvise might be the most useful skill to attain in these times (you remember the times, don't you – those fast-changing ones?).

Agile, flexible, nimble. You may have heard these words being used in business contexts (or on LinkedIn), hailed as the next best thing to transform your business. The words have lost some of their potency and have taken on the feel of marketing buzz-words or design-thinking business jargon. However, these words do still have value for us, as they share common ground in being focused on responsiveness. Ideas are reflexes. Being able to remove the barriers that allow us to react with pace to our intuition is vital for us to be able to improvise.

The ubiquitous question asked of all teachers is this: 'What should I do now?' In our experience, students often lack the confidence to adopt an open approach to uncertainty, and there are many reasons for this. The blunt answer of 'You figure it out!' might just be the best way to respond. Anything softer may inadvertently limit an individual's capacity to improvise. Teaching people to make it up as they go along might sound like an oxymoron. However, in art, life or business, focusing on our intuitive responsiveness to the unexpected can only be a good thing.

An essential function of play is to prepare us for the unexpected. Whether it's walking down the street trying to avoid the cracks, or jumping up to touch a dangling branch, creating obstacles for us to overcome is a form of playful training, and we continuously do this in our daily lives (although more so in our childhood). We will often observe these opportunities to play, and simply being receptive to them as they present themselves is the first step. However, beyond observing or being receptive to play, things start to become interesting when we actively pursue the unexpected as a part of our practice.

Brian Eno and Peter Schmidt's *Oblique Strategies* are essentially a document of this active pursuit of the unexpected in a box – literally.[8] Created through observations of their own work, the deck of over 100 cards invites the user to improvise a response to a statement or question in the light of whatever project they are working on, be it visual, textual or musical. This kind of improvisation forces us to make it up as we go along – not blindly guessing and hoping for the best, but informed by our experiences to date, and inspired by the potential offered in the new opportunity.

Work and mental health

We all have this little voice in our head that says 'Shouldn't you be working?' The pressures of work can tend to make us approach things more seriously and result in anxiety, even when it comes to simple decisions. At undergraduate level in the UK, we've seen a considerable rise in anxiety and depression. In 2013 it doubled.

Opposite:
Haydn—Lipstick, collage by Millie Burdon (see page 214 Combine)

(Similar trends can be seen in the USA and other nations with a strong work ethic as part of their culture). Several factors contribute to this: student fees, a culture where everything is quantifiable, our relationship with technology, and no doubt many more.

Simply put, work is more stressful than play, and stress stops creativity dead in its tracks. It's clear to us that play is a state that is better at encouraging creativity, so in the pursuit of new ideas, any creative individual needs to spend more time at play than at work. Why, then, isn't play more deeply ingrained in our education and business culture? The general attitude and assumptions we have about work can make the notion of play seem unprofessional, or at worst even criminal. Yet play has value in the workplace in that it can activate our creativity (give this book to your boss if they don't believe you). It can provide a platform for alternative views and perspectives on routine and common tasks we engage in every day.

As well as encouraging our imagination, we know that all aspects of play are linked to our mental health. The German poet Friedrich von Schiller described play as 'the expression of exuberant energy and the origin of all art.'[9] Essentially, play is a way of *letting off steam*.

In many of our workshops over the years we have limited the use of computers, introducing fast-paced game play and experimental persona workshops, all approached with an attitude of active and spirited playfulness. Their effects on mental health haven't yet been tracked in any quantifiable way (we're not scientists, and we've tried to create a sense of freedom in our workshops – a space free from metrics). Yet, anecdotally the results have been overwhelmingly positive. Students have gained great confidence in their practice and their ability to cooperate in a social group. One reason for this positive reaction is that play creates an experimental 'safe zone' that supports social bonding and activates peoples' seeking systems. As professor of organizational behaviour Daniel Cable explains: 'Our seeking systems create the natural impulse to explore our worlds, learn about our environments, and extract meaning from our circumstances.'[10]

Play triggers this exploration, and when we use these seeking systems, it releases dopamine in our brain (a neurotransmitter linked to motivation and pleasure), which makes us happy and makes us want to explore more. This particular habit loop is one worth repeating: play, explore (extract knowledge and meaning), release dopamine (be happy) and repeat.

Once our seeking systems are activated, we experience positive and 'persistent feelings of interest, curiosity, sensation seeking, and (in the presence of a complex cortex) the search for higher meaning' (Jaak Panksepp[11]). Approaching new situations through play, we are more open and enthusiastic about change – which limits our anxieties and apprehensions. This, in turn, allows us to create work that may not have been possible within our normal working conditions. There is no doubt, work that surprises us will bring a smile to our face. Mihaly Csikszentmihalyi, in his much-cited *Flow*, describes how a feeling of enjoyment is 'characterized by this forward movement: by a sense of novelty, of accomplishment.'[12] Achieving something unexpected or previously unimaginable brings us joy.

Not only is play good for us but it's also a useful indicator of wellbeing, and is usually the first thing to stop when someone becomes stressed, anxious, hungry or ill.[13] One can assume that if play stops due to these factors, creativity will stop too. Stress and anxiety will then stop us in our tracks when it comes to re-engaging with play and, conversely, the absence of play in one's life can contribute to a rise in anxiety. And so the vicious cycle begins. Conscious and deliberate immersion and play can short-circuit this cycle, and – although awkward to start with – quickly reintroduce the conditions needed for creativity. As a result of this (almost as a by-product), immersion and play can also be catalysts for wellbeing.

Forget the outcome. Focus on the play. (Be happy!)

Playing by (and breaking) the rules

As older children and adults, we tend to become more disciplined in our play as we add rules. Play does need some parameters, and games provide a great structure to adhere to. However, within any game, there will always be a certain degree of choice (about how we play or how we implement the rules). Think of the roles of the artist and guardian here. Setting up the game and agreeing to the rules in advance is the guardian's domain; only then can we

It's part of human nature to want to play, but once we have become boring grown-ups, we may well have forgotten how to harness the power of play.

Forget the outcome. Focus on the play.
Be happy!

play with any freedom from thought. Imagine how frustrating a game of football would be if we couldn't agree on what to do every time the ball goes out of play. The same applies to our creative practice. It's impossible to get into the flow until at least some of the parameters are determined for us (see Creative Constraints, Chapter 2).

Once we're within a game, we're following a defined pattern of play. We follow the conventions of the game-play within all rule-based games and competitive sports. This is defined as *serious play* (a term popularized by Michael Schrage in his book of the same name[14]) and is not considered to be 'playful'. *Playful play* [15] is distinct from serious play in that it's 'accompanied by a positive mood state in which an individual is more inclined to behave in a spontaneous and flexible way.'[16] Playful play, it seems, involves testing boundaries and breaking the rules.

Adopting a persona

Looking at play in more detail offers even more practical ways of enhancing our creativity. For example, the ritual of wearing a costume and entering a specific place to play is the performance of an alternative persona. It allows us to be someone else for a little while, and this performance makes us happy. The adage *dress for the job you want* may have some tangible benefits, as it's proven that the clothes we wear can affect both our physical and mental performance. This psychological improvement (called *enclothed cognition*) suggests something is happening to us biologically when we dress up. In tests, subjects were asked to perform cognitive tasks wearing formal and casual clothing. It transpired that wearing a smart suit increased the participants' abstract thinking due to increased feelings of power. Similarly, men wearing informal clothing were less able to negotiate tasks, due to having lower testosterone levels. And during simple focus-driven tasks, people made far fewer mistakes while wearing a lab coat. Famously, the Austrian composer (and one of the most influential figures in the development of Classical music during the eighteenth century) Franz Joseph Haydn couldn't achieve a mental state conducive to composing unless he dressed in full formal attire, including wig and lipstick. Each to their own. Guess it's time to rock out the old smart-suit-and-lab-coat combo (and better add a wig and lipstick too, just for good measure).

Clothing is just one example of the detail of play. We could talk more about the playing field (where), the players (who), the mechanics of the play (what) or the aim of the play (why), but then we'd have nothing to say in Chapter 4 – Practice – where we do all of this and more.

Summary

We're all in a unique position because we can choose how to be creative. We can all take ourselves (and our work) waaaay too seriously. Academia is often guilty of this, and this book is, in part, an attempt to redress the balance. Work environments, even in the creative industries, can often feel a little stuffy. People can also feel stifled by the weight of responsibility or stressed by the pressures associated with deadlines. It seems that learning is a serious business, but it doesn't need to be. And, as we've tried to explain, it's better for us if it's not. So, as a reminder:

1 | Humans need to be active and to explore. So, adopt a playful attitude towards your activity and exploration. This is as much a physical action as a mental one, so move around in both domains.

2 | An essential function of play is to prepare you for the unexpected. So focus on your intuitive responsiveness to the unexpected and be ready to improvise. Trust your intuition; trust your gut feeling.

3 | Immersion and play are great catalysts for creativity. As a result of this – almost as a by-product – they can be catalysts for our wellbeing. So, forget the outcome and focus on the play.

4 | Creative games provide a safe framework for us to develop new ideas, drawing out our natural curiosity and fostering imagination. So seek out pleasure in pattern-finding in your play.

Finally, play makes us more active, it makes us more open to exploration, it makes us laugh, and it makes us happy. So be playful and capricious, cheerful and curious, fanciful, fantastic, frisky, joyous, merry, mischievous, peculiar, spirited, spontaneous, sprightly, vivacious, whimsical and zestful.

This page: Improvisation—Adults, collage by Chris Ireland (see page 214 Combine)

Chapter 4

Practice

Chapter 4:

Practice

Although the exercises are numbered, you can use them in any order, dipping in and out as necessary.

Introduction

Chapters 1 to 3 essentially cover the theory, or at least the ideas, that have underpinned much of our thinking over recent years. However, this final chapter is the beating heart of the book, and probably the main reason you're reading it. Importantly, view each of the following exercises as you would an experiment – with an open mind and a sense of curiosity – and don't presume that the point in each case is immediately obvious.

The key to any lasting impact on your creative process is the subsequent reflection on what worked well (or otherwise). Evaluation is a critical part of each activity – something that many students forgo in favour of moving on too quickly. Most activities come with a few things for you to consider after the event – give yourself time to reflect. Growth always takes time.

The exercises are all designed in such a way that you can dip in and out and choose them in any order. They will all offer you an opportunity to view your practice from a fresh perspective, or question assumptions you may have. Nevertheless, if you're looking for a great place to start, we'd recommend the first four exercises, in order, as they build on a sequential workshop that we've run many times in the past.

01 Me! Me! Me!

Context

This exercise looks at your immediate sense of self, the things you are drawn to creatively and your thinking on the themes of identity, habit and play. It's a useful reminder of who you (really) are. Gaining a firmer grasp of key points of personal reference is incredibly helpful for creativity in general; it can also help us better understand our creative habits and tendencies.

Helps: Build personal context in defining who you are, and why.

Time: 1–3 hours+.

Tools: Pencil and paper.

Practice

Identity:

1 | Write down five things we might not know about you – the important, interesting and also more light-hearted stuff.

2 | Finish the following:

I collect:

I am passionate about:

On weekends, I:

I wish I was:

Last novel I read:

Last film I watched:

The film I've watched the most:

My signature dish:

My earliest memory:

My most prized possession:

The most exciting thing I've ever seen in real life:

The most exciting thing I've ever seen on the internet:

Below: Marine Debris typeface by Dion Star

MARINE DEBRIS TYPEFACE

Collected, unmanipulated from:
Wherrytown Beach, Penzance, Cornwall

Wherrytown Beach 36pt

ABCDEFGHIJKLMNO
PQRSTUVWXYZ
1234567890

Alternative characters

ABRAABBBCÇÇCCCCC
DFFJJ+HIIIJJJJJLLO
OPFÇSTIUVYYX

Additional characters

Above: Puncture repair kit collection by Andy Neal

Skills:

3 | What can you do? List 3 impressive things that you can do – tangible skills that sit outside your discipline.

4 | What would you like to be able to do? List 3 desired skills (e.g., coding, speaking fluent Italian, playing the piano).

Interests:

5 | If you were to deliver a 5-minute talk on a subject matter of your choice outside your discipline, what would it be?

6 | What are your other main interests?

Inspiration:

7 | Who do you admire?

8 | What are the best or most inspiring pieces of creative work you have ever seen from: an artist, designer, musician, writer, film-maker...?

9 | Who or what makes you come alive?

Above: Marine Debris, detail, Dion Star

Transition:

10 | When you were a child, what did you want to be when you grew up?

11 | What do you want to be when you (really) grow up?

List your top 3 future employers or dream jobs. Be bold.

12 | Alternatively, consider the idea of growing into a broader role.

Contemplate who you are vs what you want to be, above and beyond a job title.[1] Where else could you go?

13 | What if there were no jobs?

In a post-work world with no money, when robots are doing your laundry and all of your work is automated, how would you like to spend your time?

Reflect

Want to go further? Try Paul Thek's *Teaching Notes* (1978–1981).[2] Paul Thek was an American artist who taught at the Cooper Union School of Arts in New York. He prepared a series of questions for his graduate seminar (widely available online), which build from basic biographical prompts through to much more challenging, unusual and personal questions.

Alternatively, begin to reflect and comment on your answers to the questions above as a stream-of-consciousness response – writing and/or drawing any thoughts or ideas as they arrive. Be quick, don't overthink, and try not to edit in your head. Just record everything that comes to mind for now. This is simply a gathering exercise that tries to capture your unique perspective on the subject matter.

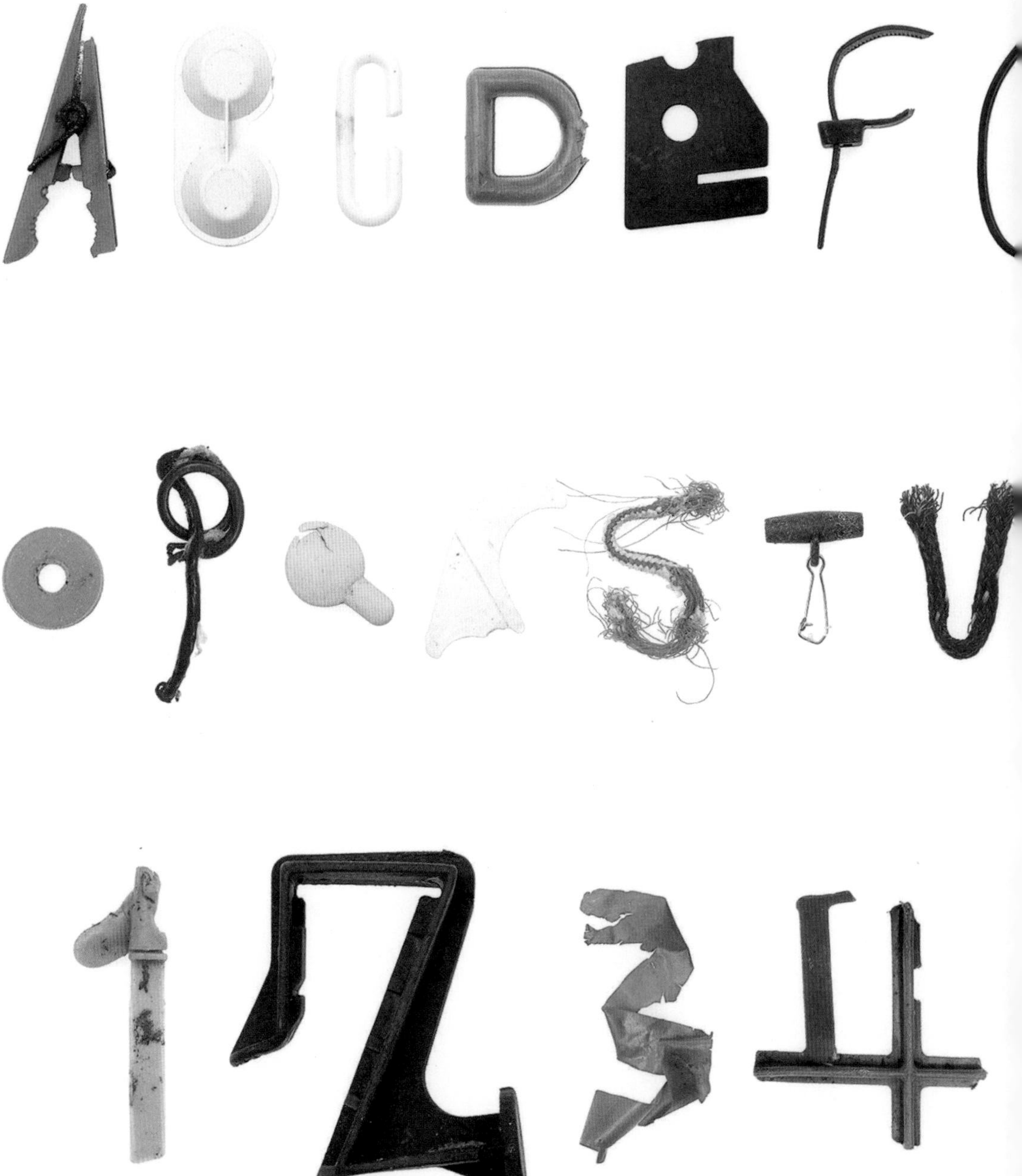

02 Frames of Reference

Context

This activity can help you to further understand your reference points (the existing cultural anchors from which you make your creative judgements) as an individual. However, it works best when collaborating in a group, as the comparison of responses is useful and often revealing – providing collective reference points (or context).

So, how do current circumstances affect our creative practice? Artists often use their environment as a site of critique or intervention. We can view their work as being about the social or political context in which it was made. Could we say the same of the work of a designer or a musician?

We all coexist and have many shared experiences, yet not all creators feel compelled to refer to their immediate context within their work. The creative choices we face are complex and demanding, and we're participating in an environment characterized by an increasing array of media, accelerated consumption, volatile political conditions, varying degrees of critical discourse...

In the face of a constant stream of instantly available published work online, via social networks or elsewhere, and with an over-reliance on increasingly common tools, it may be no surprise that our work might begin to look the same. In terms of our creativity, we respond to particular situations based on our collected and stored frames of reference, so exploring these references is an essential step in understanding where our ideas come from.

Practice

Frames of reference [3]
Produce a one-page (letter size, portrait) list that spans the last decade. Record in bullet-point form all the major public (or private) events that have made a notable impression on you,

Helps: Build a shared context in defining who you are, and why.

Time: 1–3 hours+.

Tools: Pencil, paper, sticky notes as a start.

Frames of Reference by Nina Masterton

| 2010 | Tories come into power |
| | Creation of Instagram |

2011
Christchurch earthquake
Tohuku earthquake and tsunami causing nuclear disaster in Fukushima

2012
Olympic Games in London
Attempted assassination of Malala Yousafzai in retaliation for her activism
Got my first iPhone
Lived/studied in a Buddhist temple for two weeks with a group of students

2013
Horse meat scandal
Same sex marriage law passed in UK
'twerk' and 'selfie' were added to the Oxford English Dictionary

2014
Ebola epidemic in West Africa
First involvement with a social media challenge – ice bucket challenge for ALS

2015
Charlie Hebdo incident
FCC approves net neutrality rules
Listened to Carl Sagan's audio version of his 1994 book *Pale Blue Dot*

2016
Paris Agreement on climate change
EU Referendum
Kim Kardashian robbed at gunpoint
Trump wins US election
Visited Ann Veronica Janssens's exhibition at the Wellcome Collection
Saw the Chapelle du Rosaire de Vence
One month in New Zealand

2017
Westminster and London Bridge terror attacks
Manchester Arena terrorist bombing
Grenfell Tower fire
Read *Design as Art* by Bruno Munari
Travelled to Europe after leaving secondary education

2018
Salisbury novichok attack on Russian double agent
Notre Dame fire
Entered higher education
Read *Design for the Real World* by Victor Papanek

2019
Terror attack in Christchurch Mosque, followed by legislation on firearms by Ardern
Greta Thunberg gives speech at UN summit

2020
Britain leaves the EU
Australian bushfires
Covid-19
BLM protests
Watched *The Social Dilemma* on Netflix
Three months in Japan

and any meaningful experiences you've had. Consider everything from the cultural, social and political things that have taken place across the world, through to the books, films, artworks or even personal encounters that have made a mark on you. Try to list up to 20 points in total. You can list multiple things from a particular year but do try to include at least one item for each of the years. These are some of your *frames of reference.*

If you are now 21, for example, your world has expanded and changed considerably since the age of 11. What significant things have happened around you and perhaps in some way been involved in the formation of your character? A focus on these shared experiences can help to deepen your awareness of yourself and also what connects you to others.

Make a copy of your frames of reference and share it with each of your collaborators.

If you are just starting a project together, create a timeline on the wall and pin/sticky-note each event along the timeline.

Commemorate

Choose one of the items/events from your frames of reference list, either personal or shared, and create a memorial to commemorate your individual or your collective memory of it. Your memorial could be in the form of an image, object, event, performance, or whatever you feel is appropriate.

Reflect

Acknowledging and giving space to defining our references makes us more aware of them. This, in turn, can make us more conscious of how they can elicit positive or negative bias towards our creative choices.

03 Diagnostic

Helps: Define how you think you work and how you actually work.

Time: 1–2 hours+.

Tools: Pencil, paper, sticky notes, sketchbooks and development work from 2 recent projects, smartphone or voice recorder.

Context

This set of exercises is a diagnostic tool to help you reflect on your creative practice to date. Gathering evidence of your working process and habits, alongside the definitions of your discipline, can be used as a resource for future study. Externalizing the internal is also a crucial part of the process of enabling change – so see this, in part, as laying the groundwork that will develop into a reimagined process over time.

Practice: Your habits

Ritual 1 *Allow 10 minutes*

Think about your average working day. Record answers to the following (we encourage you to both write and draw) and try to capture a real-life, warts-and-all snapshot of an average 24 hours. We're assuming there is some regular creative activity in there somewhere, so base it around that, and roll any odd details into a generic overview of you doing whatever it is you do. Be honest. Capture *now*, rather than something you are aiming for (imagine a day-in-the-life documentary, with this being the initial storyboard):

When and how do you wake up?
When and how do you go to sleep?
What daily rituals do you engage in?
Who do you see?
Where do you go?
What has to happen?
What do you try to avoid?
When are you at your peak?
When do you feel drained?
Good people?
Exhausting people?
Useful/useless tools?

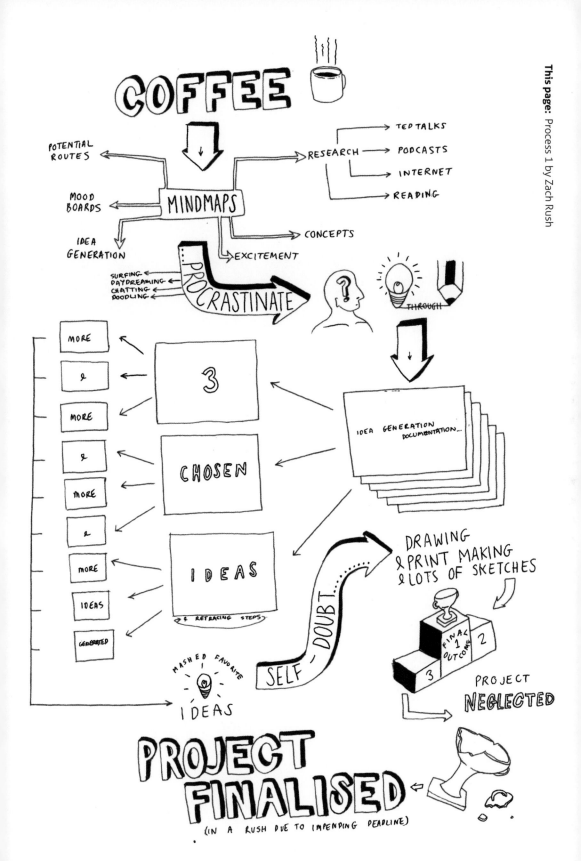

COFFEE

POTENTIAL ROUTES

MOOD BOARDS

IDEA GENERATION

MINDMAPS

RESEARCH → TED TALKS
→ PODCASTS
→ INTERNET
→ READING

CONCEPTS

EXCITEMENT

PROCRASTINATE

SURFING
DAYDREAMING
CHATTING
DOODLING

THROUGH

MORE
&
MORE
&
MORE
&
MORE
IDEAS
GENERATED

3

CHOSEN

IDEAS

& RETRACING STEPS

IDEA GENERATION DOCUMENTATION...

SELF - DOUBT

DRAWING & PRINT MAKING & LOTS OF SKETCHES

FINAL 1 OUTCOME 2
3

MASHED FAVORITE

IDEAS

PROJECT NEGLECTED

PROJECT FINALISED

(IN A RUSH DUE TO IMPENDING DEADLINE)

Habits?

Joys?

Distractions?

Critical voices?

Others...?

Collate your thoughts into a basic 24-hour flowchart from start to finish.

Ritual 2 *Allow 5 minutes*

1 | Think about the way you'd typically approach working on a brief or commission – the *normal* creative practice you engage in, from the initial conversations, through development, to ideas and production. Make some notes.

2 | Graphically translate this practice or process into a visual map or flowchart (as if someone else had followed you throughout a project and created a visual summary of what you *normally* do – a picture of how you work). Speed is the key here. Don't overthink it, and work from memory.

Practice: Your discipline

Why_____? *Allow 15 minutes*

1 | Think about your primary *creative* discipline: Why design? Why architecture? Why music? Think about why you enjoy it, and what led to your interest in it.

2 | Actively question your motivation.

3 | Draw your thoughts (no writing).

4 | Capture as many thoughts and ideas as possible in the available time. Working quickly is vital. Don't overthink things – stay intuitive.

This exercise works well in pairs. One thinking and talking, the other questioning and drawing.

This page: Illustration by Zach Rush

Practice: Your process

Process 1 *Allow 20 minutes*

1 | Brutal honesty is vital for this exercise. Spend 10 minutes going back through the sketches and notes from a recently completed project. Capture some of the critical stages, activities, questions, choices, locations, tools, people, errors, realizations as notes or sketches. This is you observing yourself at work. Use no more than the given time.

2 | Spend the next 10 minutes graphically translating this actual process into a visual map or flowchart that records what you did *for real* during that project – from start to finish. A to B. Just go for top-line observations. Don't get caught up in too much detail, unless it's significant.

Optional: You may wish to repeat this exercise for a second project, perhaps one that is different to the first – so a commercial brief vs a personal one, a short one vs a long one, open-ended vs specific, etc.

Process 2 (essence) *Allow 10 minutes*
Create a list of 6 to 10 verbs that accurately represent your existing creative process. Again, be honest with yourself (this is vital).

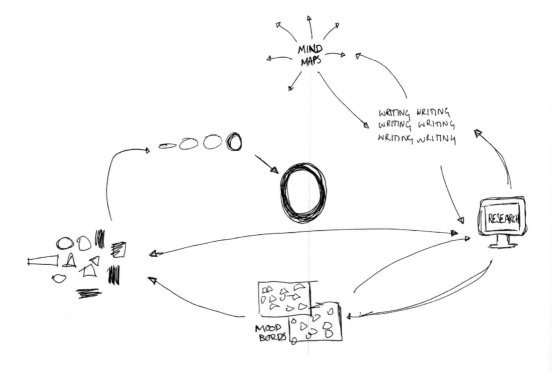

Practice: Definitions

Allow 15 minutes

1 | Record yourself describing your subject (design, architecture, music, etc.) to a group of imaginary, but interested, teenagers. You have no rehearsal, and only 2 minutes to complete the task. Don't stop to re-record and don't prepare in any way. Consider the following in your response: What is it? Why is it important? Why should they care?

2 | Having recorded the description, play it back to yourself *once.* Just listen.

3 | Now summarize your comments as a series of written notes and drawn sketches on some sticky notes.

4 | Look back over your sketches. Are there any themes or patterns? It can be helpful to arrange the sticky notes thematically.

5 | Is there anything obvious missing? Does anything surprise you (other than the sound of your voice!)? Add to the notes as appropriate.

This exercise works well in pairs or threes as a discussion with no note-taking. Complete the subsequent reflections as individuals, capturing as much of the conversation from memory as you can.

04 Warrior Mode
(pick a fight – with yourself)

Context

Everything we do creatively will exist within a context. We all tend to stick with what we know, and this can become a significant problem. Fear of change, creative bias, blind spots and so on are all factors that can quietly limit our capacity to grow.

We all have a backstory, a history that shapes the existing expression of our craft (our unique manifesto, if you like) – the *me*. Beyond histories and manifestos, there is *us* – the *we*, the collective creative voice, and its capacity to shape our thinking more subtly. Thirdly, there are our individual and collective habits – the interplay of behaviours that shape our practice at a far deeper level and are often harder to identify or change. These themes all coalesce into a broad but ultimately limited framework, and it's essential to be aware of this before we move on.

In encouraging our students to identify their existing practice, and to then move beyond it, we have tried several approaches – from a step-by-step, incremental evolution to a more dramatic thrown-in-at-the-deep-end revolution. What works best comes down to each individual's preferences. However, just like easing yourself slowly into icy water rather than swiftly taking the plunge, the evolution route brings with it a prolonged discomfort – sometimes even to the point where you reject any lasting change in favour of the known and familiar (or you decide to forgo a swim altogether!). By contrast, throwing yourself in quickly (the revolution) creates a bigger shock to the system. However, unlike the risk of a heart attack in the case of a freezing lake, dramatic, creative change seems to unlock a legitimate, and positive, shift in behaviour – short-circuiting what exists already, and opening up new possibilities.

As part of our work exploring ways to address the evolution/revolution balance – and particularly the belief that

Helps: Embrace a radically different way of working.

Time: 3–6 hours+.

Tools: Pencil, paper, material from exercises 1, 2 and (particularly) 3, plus a current brief.

revolution can create more significant results – this playful and practical activity has been successful in opening up alternative perspectives and possibilities. So if you are feeling any inertia when it comes to creative change, this is for you.

Practice

Warrior Mode 1 (pick a fight)
Allow 60 minutes (although it can take much longer)

1 | Start with your list of verbs from Process 2 in Diagnostic (pp. 92–97), or if you haven't completed that exercise yet, create a list of 6 to 10 verbs that accurately represent your existing creative process. It's key to be honest with yourself.

2 | Now, the FIGHT! Systematically pick each word apart and propose dramatic alternatives (opposites, antonyms, alternative experiences) to each of them. Use a thesaurus to help you. Aim for direct opposites where possible.

3 | Reorder these alternative words as you see fit to create a new list. This list of words is your new Warrior Mode process. There is no right or wrong. Just go for an extreme and trust your instincts. (This list should act as a series of clear instructions or a flowchart that someone else could follow when next given a creative problem to wrestle with.)

4 | Give your Warrior Mode a name (perhaps one from your list) that accurately describes the spirit of your inner warrior. Add this to the top of the list.

5 | Pin your Warrior Mode list to the wall.

'How much can you know about yourself if you've never been in a fight.'

Chuck Palahniuk[4]

Warrior Mode 2 (action)
Allow 120 minutes

1 | Consider an existing brief (or a problem you are trying to find solutions for).

2 | Use your Warrior Mode process to respond to it. It's highly likely that your new process will be impractical, illogical and even impossible to execute fully. However, the point is to force yourself to use a creative process that's mostly set up to fail and to reflect on how it makes you behave.

3 | Generate as much as you can in the way of material, thoughts, possibilities and ideas in the available time.

Below: Warrior Mode workshop

Warrior Mode 3 (reflection)

Allow 30 minutes

Sometimes we get stuck in a creative rut and, no matter how hard we try, we can't get out of it. We can all end up in fruitless working loops (doing things the same way, consciously and subconsciously) at any stage of development – beginner to seasoned pro. When this happens, doing nothing new will give you nothing new. Doing the exact opposite will, at the very least, force a new approach into the mix. You may even find that your Warrior Mode provides surprising results or perhaps gives you a fresh perspective, and it will always be something you need to invest in and refine.

Importantly, we've seen that by embracing a radically new way to react to a problem (even if it's verging on the ridiculous), you can open up to a

Below: Warrior Mode maze (detail) by Ellie Powell

range of new possibilities scattered between your normal practice and its warrior opposite.

There is the old commercial-design adage: if you want to get your client to move from 1 to 2, show them 3 first. If your Warrior Mode is too extreme, you can still rein it in a peg or two and have something useable. At the very least, it will allow you to stop overthinking and taking yourself or your practice so seriously. The exercise encourages risk, play and failure, and as we explained in Chapter 3, these are crucial to our development.

Reflect

- Think about the process of creating your Warrior Mode.
- Did it come easily, or did you have to fight for it?
- How did you feel knowing that you were going to apply it practically?
- How useful were the outcomes?
- What would you change about the exercise if you were to do it again?
- What can you integrate into your normal practice to encourage more risk?
- Consider the progression of exercises A, B and C and how it relates to your process.

If you are working as part of a group, pick another person's Warrior Mode and respond to your brief again. Repeat until you run out of energy!

05 Library Book Persona

Context

The term *persona* has many different interpretations, traversing a wide variety of disciplines and practices (including performance, music, UX design, marketing, psychology…). In essence, we refer to it here as the way we present ourselves to others, or the way our character is perceived by those around us. A persona can be brutally honest and true to who you really are, or entirely fabricated – a fictional construct designed to conceal. Indeed, *persona* comes from the Greek term for 'mask'.

Eminent psychologist Carl Jung talked about the relationship between our persona and our longer-term psychological development.[5] If our persona is *flexible* (not tied to a specific mask and adaptable over time), we are more likely to navigate the complexities and demands of life successfully. However, a persona that relates solely to a specific role runs the risk of our becoming that persona, almost to the exclusion of everything else – a *brittle* personality.

Any creative practice therefore carries with it the danger that we become the *role* itself as we play out a predetermined set of characteristics. This is particularly true within an educational system that is quick to define us as a role: *product designer* or *documentary photographer* (terms often only useful at the recruitment end of the educational wedge). We can become the archetype of whatever we study and, in doing so, become bound by the perceived edges of its definition (increasingly so, as we progress in our career).

Creativity, however, is not bound by discipline, and our capacity to grow beyond any predetermined category is intrinsically linked to what Jung alludes to as a healthy, deep, flexible and adventurous persona. With all this in mind, spending time considering your persona as an adaptable thing should be a positive activity for both your creative practice and your psychological wellbeing.

Helps: Develop a systematic and flexible way of adopting new working methods.

Time: 2–3 days+.

Tools: Pencil, paper, access to a library, a current project.

Allan Kaprow Curated by Chloe Rendells

Key words:

> ## Physical
> ## Anti-Art
> ## Transient

1 | Go and observe people and their interactions with their surroundings/environment.

2 | Immerse yourself in philosophy, plays, poems, theatre and art about interaction and relationships.

3 | Explore/devise/create with your body and natural materials. How do you interact? How can you interact?

Quotes:

"Shedding the conventions of art in order to have unfettered experiences of life."

"Experiment with increasingly intimate forms of physical, social and psychological exchange."

"Physically and sensually present in the moment of enactment: as spaces, materials, actions, processes, encounters and the like."

Richard Long Curated by Lucy Bristow

Key words:

Simplicity
Transience
Scale

1 | Go for a walk in nature and see everything as something to be inspired by.
2 | Use your own hands as much as possible.
3 | Allow your process to be a journey, to let it adapt and change according to new influences.

Quotes:

"I like being an opportunist. I need the element of chance."

"I have to be in the moment so I don't fall off the path."

"...it wouldn't interest anyone else, but it interests me."

Daniel Eatock Curated by Samuel Clothier

Key words:

Dilemmas
Wit
Tinker

1 | Employ a rational, logical and pragmatic approach.
2 | Be engaged with the elements.
3 | Trust the process.

Quotes:

"Allow concepts to determine form."

"Celebrate coincidence."

"Be first or last."

Practice

Part 1: Source *15–30 minutes*
Go to a library and find a book on an artist/designer/photographer/etc. you're not familiar with. It must contain a mixture of written material (quotes, interviews, information about their working environment) and visual material (designs, paintings, photographs, sketches). If you struggle to find this in a single book, use additional books to complement the first (artist/designer monographs are ideal). Don't overthink this, and work within the time given.

Part 2: Filter *90–120 minutes*
Look through your book for any references to their creative process, no matter how random or tenuous. Look at how they do what they do. What motivates them? What practices do they adopt? What tools do they use? Influences? Materials? Spaces? It's unlikely that you'll find a single definitive explanation. Rather, you'll have to piece together disparate elements of a continually unfolding puzzle to find (at best) a loose approximation. Record these as a collection of words/sketches/images in the available time.

Part 3: Process *90–120 minutes*
Finally, choose one original painting/sculpture/design/photograph from the book and imagine the process of creating it – from conception through production, delivery and consumption. Record and refine this as a flowchart. Use as much detail as your imagination will allow.

Part 4: Extract *90–120 minutes*
Translate your thoughts from Parts 1, 2 and 3 so that they're in a form that could be understood by someone else wishing to adopt this working practice. This must include (as a minimum):

- 3 direct instructions.
- 3 images that capture the spirit of their thinking or work.
- 3 quotes that frame their thinking, ideologies, perspective, etc.
- 3 keywords that capture the spirit of their practice.

Part 5: Adopt a persona *1 day*

Using your new persona, adopt and 'wear' the working process (or mask) for a project that you're currently developing (or have recently finished). The trick here is not to focus on getting great ideas to *solve* the problem in hand, or indeed to create a tangible outcome at all. The aim, rather, is to explore and adopt a different way of working to see where it leads. You should be consciously refining your understanding of this new process as you're working – don't slip back into the real you (not yet). This will feel unfamiliar and uncomfortable but it will begin to offer new perspectives and pathways. Pay particular attention to anything that creates some kind of reaction in you, and regularly refer back to the guidelines given in Part 4.

Reflect

The beauty of this activity is that you can repeat it as often as you like, with as many new masks as you have the energy to embrace. We've seen students systematically consume a diverse range of personas over several months – deliberately stepping out of their practice, embracing entirely new ways of working, and seeing a significant development in their conceptual breadth as a consequence. Equally, others have chosen to focus in detail on their existing discipline, exploring the subtleties and nuances of their craft and thereby increasing their depth of understanding significantly. The beauty of all of these exercises is that we have no idea if the imagined list of behaviours represents the actual creative practice of the individual concerned. They can, at best, only ever be approximations, and at the end of the day, diversity (rather than accuracy) is the goal. By embracing the variety of practices on offer, your creativity will ultimately become more profound, flexible and adventurous.

Isabelle Cornaro Curated by Rebecca James

Key words:

Representation
Abstract
Allegory

1 | Look at different social, historical, locational contexts. How might this form a story?

2 | Find objects or inspiration in your direct environment. Collect and categorize them to create a meaning.

3 | Make things abstract rather than literal representations.

Quotes:

"Change the frame of representation."

"I like the idea of allegory, since it describes an abstract relationship to the world."

"Emotional, sentimental, but also historical and social dimensions of objects we encounter daily."

06 20–20–20

Context

We recommended using the 20–20–20 method to kickstart any creative brief, and we suggest completing this exercise in one day. The three stages – quick research, framing a brief, fast idea generation – all focus on one fundamental principle: the importance of giving yourself multiple options.

Practice

20 questions

Choose a subject area of interest to you. For this chosen subject, answer (write and draw) the 20 questions below in as much detail as possible. Unearth information and make it visible. Reveal an insight. Find an interesting story to tell. Go as wide and as deep as possible, and document as much information as you can in the time you have.

1 | What is it?
2 | How do we find it?
3 | Who are the experts in this subject?
4 | Where can you experience it?
5 | How might people research it?
6 | What is its history?
7 | How would you define its purpose?
8 | Who might be interested in this? (Define the audience.)
9 | What does it sound like?
10 | What does it feel like?
11 | Can you describe its attitude?
12 | If it was an object, what would it be?
13 | What emotions are related to it?
14 | How do you measure it?
15 | How would you describe its personality?
16 | How many different ways can you experience it?
(Think channels of communication.)

17 | What unique language does it use?

18 | What terminology or slang would it use?

19 | Is it local or global?

20 | Where is it going? (What will it look like in the future?)

20 briefs

What is interesting? What insight is important? Analyse the raw materials you've gathered and write 20 questions about the subject. Think of these as *one-sentence briefs*. Consider framing your brief as follows:

How might we communicate: <insert something>
in the context of: <insert context>
through: <insert medium>
for: <insert audience>

Or, simply:
How might we communicate* X in the context of Y?

challenge, reduce, enhance, express, rethink, share, revolutionize, champion the importance of, convince people of, create a tangible, engage with, change the perception of, celebrate the diversity of, better connect with, innovate in the field of, radically evolve, etc.

Some questions to help you write your one-sentence brief:
• What problem are you trying to solve?
• What's the impact you're trying to have?
• What's the context?
• What are the constraints?
• What can we do to make a difference?
• Why is it important to you?
• Who are you talking to and what do you want them to do, think or feel?

20 ideas

Once you have 20 potential briefs, pick one (at random if you have to). Respond to this brief and try to generate as many ideas as possible. Stop at 20. By getting one idea, you at least have a response. Three, you'll be able to make judgements on which one is stronger. By ten, you'll be starting to understand the nuances required to make the best idea better. By generating 20, or more, you'll start seeing patterns in your thinking, and your best idea will probably have several unique expressions – all of which could potentially work.

Some questions to focus your ideas:
- What is it?
- What does it do?
- Why does it matter?
- Why is this important to you?
- Why is this important to others?

Make

Now choose an idea and make it. Develop your idea into something that communicates an insight from your chosen subject in a compelling way. The format for your proposal is to be determined by you. It could be an object, an interaction, an experience, a single image or series of images. The choice is entirely yours – just make sure it brings your subject to life and involves or engages your audience in some way.

Below: One-day project by Kyra Marks: hand-made wrapping paper for a heart disease charity (celebrating the insight that potatoes support heart health)

07 The Edit Switch

Context

We reflected on the idea of editing, conceptual freefall and the delicate balance between the two in Chapter 1. We also referenced the notion that we cannot control creativity – all we can do is try to *harness* it. The analogy is of your guardian reconfiguring and presenting information to your artist in such a way as to allow new creative combinations to occur (Chapter 2). This exercise explores the notion of harnessing two states that can help (or hinder, if avoided) the development of our ideas.

Consider your thinking as being consciously governed by a metaphorical switch – a simple two-way A/B device that flips to one or other of those states at any given moment in time. When the switch is flipped to state A, *flow*, we are free to imagine new possibilities, to explore creativity and to experiment. Flow = quantity. Anything is possible. Everything is in. What if...? And so on. Conversely, when the switch is flipped to state B, *filter*, we're looking back critically at the material we've collated in the flow state and making judgements about its appropriateness and effectiveness. Filter = quality. What works? What do I like? What challenges conventions? Both of these states (A/B) are expressions of our guardian controlling the way that our artist responds to a given task, with a strategic goal in mind – that of developing more creative ideas.

The real challenge here (and the thing we often miss) is in allowing the edit switch to stay in the flow state for any length of time. We tend to default to the filter state, making dismissive choices and rejecting ideas in milliseconds. However, we have seen the Edit Switch work well, as it celebrates both the flow of conceptual freefall, and the filter of editing as equally important. They need each other. It is also a visual tool that seems to work well within creative fields, and the metaphor evolves the more you work with it.

(When) to edit, or (when) not to edit. That is the question.

Practice

A number of the other exercises (Translation on pp. 198–201 and Combine on pp. 214–217, in particular) encourage you to dwell in the flow state as a by-product of that specific exercise. There are also other well-known lateral-thinking exercises (how many uses for a paper clip can you think of in 5 minutes[6], for example, or De Bono's Green 'Creative' Hat[7]), which all try to encourage the same good practice. As with all of the exercises in this chapter, use the following as a starting point – actively looking to adjust and refine each section to suit your own goals. Importantly, becoming familiar with how each state *feels* (the conscious awareness of its unique qualities) is essential, as we can easily drift from one to the other without realizing it.

Part 1: Build

The strength of the Edit Switch is in your ownership of each state, and its relationship to your specific craft:

1 | Create a list of alternative words for the flow and filter states (use a thesaurus and your imagination). Be mindful of your specific discipline and any language that may be more/less appropriate. Don't rush this. Consider how you work, and look for words/phrases that relate to you and to your way of thinking.

Flow	Filter
Off	On
Quantity	Quality
Possibility	Potential
Divergent	Convergent
Etc.	Etc.

2 | Now think about the materials, tools and symbolism of your discipline – the visual vernacular of your craft. Write a list. Create a mood board. Draw or collage key elements (whatever works best for you).

3 | Finally, draw, design and then make your physical Edit Switch incorporating language and materials that best relate to you and your craft. This could be as simple as the two key states written and pinned on your wall, through to a complex automaton with levers and pulleys that's given a permanent place on your desk. The switch is simply a totem of your intentions, though, rather than possessing the need for any literal functionality – it is only a metaphor, after all.

Part 2: Test

Now, with a current project, consider the following (and have your physical switch to hand – just for moral support):

1 | Identify a question or problem that needs a response within your work.

2 | Set a timer for 2 minutes.

3 | Set your Edit Switch to *flow* (anything is possible, everything is in, what if...) then write and/or draw as many themes/ideas/words/images/metaphors related to your question as you can in the available time. You must record *every* thought, and herein lies the discipline. Good, bad, relevant, random, abstract, ridiculous, plain stupid – all possibilities are valid at this stage. Do *not* edit; every connection, thought or idea has potential, no matter how obscure. Be mindful that editing often occurs at a subconscious level, so actively look to enter a state of flow. Aim for volume rather than quality – how many can you think of in 2 minutes.

4 | When the time is up, then (and only then) set your Edit Switch to *filter*.

5 | Reflect on your thinking and identify viable responses for further development: What has potential? What do I like? What challenges conventions? What is surprising? And so on...

Repeat the exercise at regular intervals, gradually increasing the available time to freefall as a regular practice: 2 minutes, 5 minutes, 10 minutes, 30 minutes and finally 60 minutes. Beyond an hour, the process can become too exhausting (see Passive/Active p. 156), and we'd encourage you to take a break.

Part 3: Feedback

We talked about the artist/guardian metaphor and its use in our teaching in Chapter 2 (p. 50). We've also just used it as a practical exercise – forming the basis of the Edit Switch to build regular critique into every activity you engage with. In the following exercise, it simply provides a framework to locate your flow/filter thinking, but adds the idea of a feedback loop, making the process more cyclical:

1 | Draw a line down a piece of paper (or use two facing pages in a sketchbook). Write ARTIST in the left column/page, and GUARDIAN in the right.

Artist	Guardian

2 | Set a timer and then enter the *flow* state, encouraging your artist to play undisturbed and uninterrupted until your time is up. Record all this thinking on the artist side of the page.

3 | When you switch to the *filter* state, your guardian is critiquing the play and identifying ideas with potential. Record all this thinking on the guardian side of the page. The key difference is at this point, when you then return to your flow/artist state and re-engage with the play, you do so in light of your guardian's observations.

This feedback loop allows you to continue switching between flow/filter, artist/guardian for as long as you have the energy – honing and refining your thinking as you go. Over time, the visual distance (left/right of the page) between your flow and filter thinking can become a useful tool for reflecting on your work.

Reflect

Parts 2 and 3 look specifically at the development of ideas, and this final part looks at using your guardian as a reflective tool, considering the whole process you are going through – in other words, the success (or otherwise) of your Edit Switch. It provides an objective critique of how you are progressing, offering an opportunity to adjust and improve the process for your long-term gain. You can transpose this exercise to any of the exercises in this chapter – or indeed, any practical, creative activity.

Stepping back from the tasks above, consider the whole Edit Switch experience in the light of your guardian self (objective, organized, practical, considered, intellectual...). You will have your own questions (and will develop more over time), but here are some to get you going:

• Did the exercise(s) protect your artist's ability to play?
• Where was this most pronounced?
• What could you do to improve the task(s)?
• What issue(s) did it raise?
• What might need to change?
• How can you help further nurture your artist?
• What needs protecting?
• What needs removing?

As with any attempt to change a behaviour, or work through a (bad) habit, we need to identify and accept that there's something we wish to change. We need to understand the contributing factors and triggers, put tangible steps in place to offer an alternative course of action, and then apply these – ensuring we maintain them over time. Discipline is central to all of these stages, as it's rare for any of us to change patterns of behaviour overnight.

Training our creative selves to slow down – consciously creating space to allow ideas to flow without restraint, and to then (and only then) critique them in the light of predetermined goals – is at odds with many of the dualistic processes we are taught as children. Building in the discipline of flow/filter takes time and effort but can be a significant factor in seeing your creativity mature.

08 Desire Lines

Helps: Identify and utilize areas of creative potential.

Time: 1–6 hours+.

Tools: Pencil and paper.

Context

Desire line: 'a path created as a consequence of erosion caused by human or animal foot traffic. The path usually represents the shortest or most easily navigated route between an origin and destination. The width and severity of erosion are often indicators of the traffic level that a path receives. Desire paths emerge as shortcuts where constructed paths take a circuitous route, have gaps, or are non-existent.' [8]

Desire lines reveal the fault in the original design.

The concept of desire lines, or desire paths, has been used as an analysis tool in urban planning, to study the choices commuters make about their travel on foot, rail and subway. The term pops up in software design, too. For example, users of Twitter, attempting to overcome the limitations of the software, established various approaches – including @ mentions, hashtags and group discussions – that were then later integrated, in part, into the service.

Within education we can often spend years gaining a grounding in one subject, only to realize towards the end of our study that we want to spend much more of our time in another.

In our years of teaching design, we've noticed that each year a handful of students will realize that they wish to shift their focus to (for example) photography, illustration or animation. Either they've fallen out of love with the original discipline, or they initially chose it due to their skill or interest in one aspect of the subject, but were then guided more by an external influence (parent, tutor, etc.) than by their own heart. When this happens, it can leave them feeling like they never got the chance to fully explore that original interest in detail, and it's often the result of having *waited for permission*.

Practice

Sometimes we need an excuse to get on with the thing we desperately want to do. The following exercise is that excuse. Where do you really want to go? What do you really want to do with your time? Who are the people you really want to collaborate with? We can sometimes feel it's too indulgent to ask these questions, especially when we consider the variety of cultural and financial pressures we often face. But if *you* can't indulge in pursuing *your* creative desires, who will?

Part 1

1 | Create three vertical columns on a large sheet of paper, then use these three themes as a heading at the top of each column:

| **Places** | **Activities** | **People** |

2 | Compile a list of places, activities and people you'd *really* like to have the opportunity to work with. Dream big. Be honest. Listen to your heart.

3 | Now draw some linking desire lines between a place, an activity and a person in an attempt to find a way to combine some of the examples from each category.

4 | Repeat this for as many combinations as makes sense.

Part 2

1 | Look at all the possible connections you have made and pick two combinations that stand out, for whatever reason.

2 | Conceive a project that combines these linked desires.

3 | Plan the *what, how* and *when* of the most exciting of the two.

4 | Get on with it! We give you our permission.

PLACES	PEOPL
hospital	students f
Falmouth	ell
Bristol	(actors) dra
my room	Thu
Australia	
markets	
cities	Wes
night time	(personal project) M
fields	
campus	
studio	C
museums	
rental space	u
national trusts	
antique shops	a
newsagents	
house	
art gallery	
Bath	
coffee shop	b

ACTIVITIES

r departments
ple
ents
rs

making sound
saving
film photography
doodling
make a publication
a short film
lino printing
social change project
social experiments
using materials
imagination
abstract
dada-esque fun project
painting
phone project
(centralises around)
make an app
(challenges) task based
short film

on

ens
l

y
s

alker

y
c
am
nia
stone

09 Mind Wandering
(Tidy House, Tidy Mind)

Helps: Identify states of mind conducive to your creativity.

Time: 2 hours+.

Tools: Pencil, paper and a pre-existing creative challenge.

Context

Have you ever wondered why your best ideas come to you in the shower? It may be a cliché, but there are reasons for this. One of them is the notion that distraction allows the mind to wander. Consciously focusing on a problem can sometimes undermine creativity. By contrast, distraction can enhance it; the brain is more capable of making lateral connections if it has engaged in a non-demanding task beforehand. Mind wandering is strongly linked to enhanced creativity, so engaging in simple, mundane tasks that allow the mind to wander may facilitate creative problem-solving, particularly with problems that have been encountered beforehand.

Practice

Part 1: Mind wandering experiment

For these exercises, you will be generating ideas in response to something you are working on, so be ready with a defined question or brief. Try to view this as an experiment (accepting risk and failure as a critical part of the experience) and attempt the following either individually or in groups to see what works best for you.

There are three different activities: meditation, cleaning, mathematics. You will spend 5 minutes performing one of the tasks, then another 5 minutes generating ideas in response to something you are working on.

- 5 minutes: Meditation (sit and do nothing)
- 5 minutes: Idea generation
- Take a break

'It will come to you when you are least expecting it – while shaving, or bathing, or most often when you are half-awake in the morning. It may waken you in the middle of the night.'

James Webb Young here – not talking about the Bogeyman, but about the arrival of new ideas.[9]

- 5 minutes: Non-demanding tasks (cleaning windows, floors, tidying, etc.)
- 5 minutes: Idea generation
- Take a break

- 5 minutes: Demanding tasks (maths equations, complicated puzzles, crosswords, sudoku, etc.)
- 5 minutes: Idea generation
- Take a break

Part 2: Mind wandering method

Before you begin an idea-generation session, we've found that it helps to be well rested and in a relaxed state. In addition to engaging with these activities in isolation, we've also seen students respond well to them as a series – running one method into the next and then moving on to develop ideas as the final stage. You may well choose to change the order to suit your own preference. Or even adapt the tasks based on your experiences above (inventing new meditation routines or non-demanding tasks). However, in our experience, the following can produce the best results:

- Read your brief or question
- 20 minutes: Meditation (sit and do nothing; try to clear your mind entirely)
- 20 minutes: Non-demanding task (cleaning, tidying, etc.)
- 20 minutes: Idea generation

Reflect

After you've performed all of the tasks, you can then reflect (individually or as a group) on which activity helped you best prepare for creating ideas. To do this, evaluate all of the ideas you've produced, in terms of:

• Fluency (number of ideas)
• Flexibility (different perspectives/fields the ideas came from)
• Originality (has anyone else thought of this?)

If these exercises are making some sense, you may wish to explore the theories underpinning them further in *Inspired by Distraction* by Benjamin Baird et al.[10]

10 Mind Wandering
(Jigsaw)

Context

We have trialled many different expressions of 'mind wandering' (deliberately allowing your conscious brain to drift in an attempt to broaden your creative thinking) – some with significant success, and others less so. What's been most interesting through this process, however, is that on nearly every occasion someone has always benefited from the experience (even if the larger group were less convinced). What appears as a success for one will undoubtedly mean frustration for another, as we creatively develop in very different ways. Exploring and defining your own version of the mind-wandering principle is perhaps the most important lesson you can take away from this exercise. That said, in our pursuit of an ever-increasing number of the predominantly successful expressions of the principle, the following method has been particularly popular.

Practice

1 | Source a jigsaw puzzle (1000 pieces+). Charity/thrift stores are a great place to look if you don't have one already, and the subject matter is (in our experience) less important than the following point.

2 | Arrange the jigsaw where you can work in peace – ideally, somewhere with ample wall-space close by and, if possible, away from your normal desk (assuming you have one).

3 | You'll need a good supply of sticky notes and a pencil.

4 | Leave the jigsaw until you have a creative challenge to work on.

Helps: Utilize absent-minded distraction as a creative tool.

Time: 1 hour+.

Tools: Pencil, sticky notes and a 1,000+ piece jigsaw puzzle.

A Fictional Book

Mind Wandering & Cognitive Drift

A.Neal & D.Star

5 | When you are feeling a little stuck, possibly at the beginning of a new project (when you are just figuring out what's required), or part way through (when you are struggling with ideas), engage with the puzzle.

6 | The exercise works best when you commit to the jigsaw for a reasonable length of time (15–20 minutes is generally good), as your brain seems to need time to settle before the subconscious kicks in.

7 | While you're trying to find a corner, or an edge, or a piece of sky, allow your mind to quietly linger on your current project. Don't try and force ideas deliberately – the whole point is one of distraction. Your conscious mind is focused on the puzzle, leaving your subconscious brain free to wander, explore and make connections you might otherwise miss.

8 | There is no limit to how long/short a time you spend with the puzzle. Just stay there to distract yourself, and to let your subconscious lead.

9 | Importantly, record any thoughts on the sticky notes as they appear, but don't dwell on them. If they become the focus, you've missed the object of the exercise. Put the note on the wall, and get back to the puzzle.

10 | DO NOT edit any potential ideas as they arrive. Simply capture them and get back to the puzzle (see the Edit Switch, pp. 116–121).

11 | When you have a reasonable number of notes/ideas, only then start editing again at your normal working desk.

Reflect

This exercise can effectively be replaced with any repetitive task, as our brains will quickly move past the immediacy of the activity – adopting the routine behaviour, and creating subconscious space to drift. We all have personal preferences when it comes to the perfect distraction, and finding yours is part of the fun.

'Creativity is just connecting things. When you ask creative people how they did something, they feel a little guilty because they didn't really do it, they just saw something. It seemed obvious to them after a while. That's because they were able to connect experiences they've had and synthesize new things.'

Steve Jobs[11]

11 Random Nouns

Helps: Utilize literal and lateral thinking to develop new ideas.

Time: 1–4 hours+.

Tools: Pencil, paper, sticky notes.

Context

Random word stimulation is a well-known lateral-thinking technique and a practical method of generating new ideas, fast. The process helps you to access existing subconscious knowledge and simply forms an association between your current theme of study and a disconnected word. You can literally pick words at random (as the title implies) by opening up a book and pointing to any word, and there are random-word generators online.

However, this does raise the question of whether all words are equal when using this method. Any success or failure is ultimately down to the given context (which you can control) and the random word selected (which you can't), but some types of words do seem to work better than others. Grammar classifies a language's lexicon into several groups of words (noun, verb, adjective, pronoun, preposition, etc.). Or, to simplify further, the fundamental binary division possible for virtually every natural language is that of nouns vs verbs: *things* and *actions*.

To generate ideas quickly, we tend (initially) to encourage the use of nouns (things), as this will trigger common symbols in the mind, with which we're likely to have multiple, varied associations, helping with the subsequent idea development.

Practice

Part 1: Generate
Define a problem for which you wish to generate solutions. Then begin by choosing a random noun. (Use the lists on the next pages.)

1 | Write down your first, immediate response to this random word. Look for a direct connection.

2 | Next, write down a second response to the word. This time, try to differentiate from the first response to create an indirect connection.

3 | Finally, write down a third response to the word (differentiate again) as a lateral connection.

Repeat the exercise, trying to differentiate more than once with the same word. The following provides an example:

Subject	Bird (1st attempt)	Bird (2nd attempt)
Direct	Wings	Nest
Indirect	Air	Flap
Lateral	Twitter	KFC

Now you have six responses to the subject/word (seven words in total).

Part 2: Ideas are reflexes

Now, generate as many ideas or connections as possible in response to your seven words. Moving from each word in the order that you wrote them down, try to link them with your defined problem. It's best not to move on to the next word until you have documented an idea for the current word. Aim to come up with an idea of any quality, but don't edit or evaluate your ideas – the task is to make a connection and loosen your thinking, not to create a fantastic solution. This easy exercise increases the scope for creating new ideas, simply by walking towards a subject from a randomly generated word.

Reflect

Once complete (and this shouldn't take too long), look at your ideas. You may have come up with a good one if you're lucky, but most likely, they will be inappropriate or underwhelming. What is important, however, is to note the perspective of the ideas you have generated. Have any come from a position you find unexpected or surprising? How can you build on this? Which words were useful to you in this exercise and which were not? Can you group similar words or ideas? Does this help?

Exhibition

Identity

Filter

Deletion

Villain

Factual

Emotional

Actor

Uprising

Lamp

Fork

Spectacles

Adult	Brain	Desk	Fruit
Aeroplane	Bridge	Diagonal	Fungus
Air	Butterfly	Diamond	Game
Airforce	Button	Dress	Garden
Airport	Cappuccino	Drill	Gas
Album	Car	Drift	Gate
Alphabet	Carpet	Drink	Gemstone
Apple	Carrot	Drum	Girl
Arm	Cave	Dung	Gloves
Army	Chair	Ears	God
Baby	Chess board	Earth	Gold
Backpack	Chief	Egg	Grapes
Balloon	Child	Electricity	Guitar
Banana	Chisel	Elephant	Hammer
Bank	Chocolates	Eraser	Hat
Barbecue	Church	Explosive	Hieroglyph
Base	Circle	Eyes	Hole
Bathroom	Circus	Family	Horoscope
Bathtub	Clock	Fan	Horse
Bed	Clown	Feather	Hose
Bee	Coal	Festival	Ice-cream
Bible	Coffee shop	Film	Insect
Bird	Comet	Finger	Jet fighter
Bomb	Compact disc	Fire	Junk
Book	Compass	Floodlight	Kaleidoscope
Boss	Computer	Flower	Kitchen
Bottle	Crystal	Foam	Knife
Bowl	Cup	Foot	Leather jacket
Box	Cycle	Fork	Leg
Boy	Database	Frame	Library

Light	Pillow	School	Teeth
Liquid	Plane	Sex	Telescope
Magnet	Planet	Ship	Television
Man	Pocket	Shoes	Tennis racquet
Map	Poor	Shop	Thermometer
Maze	Portrait	Shower	Tiger
Meat	Post office	Signature	Toilet
Meteor	Potato	Skeleton	Tongue
Microscope	Printer	Slave	Torch
Milk	Prison	Snail	Torpedo
Milkshake	Puppet	Software	Train
Mist	Pyramid	Solid	Treadmill
Money	Radar	Space shuttle	Triangle
Monster	Rainbow	Spectrum	Tribe
Mosquito	Record	Sphere	Tunnel
Mouth	Restaurant	Spice	Typewriter
Nail	Rifle	Spiral	Umbrella
Navy	Ring	Spoon	Vacuum
Necklace	Robot	Sports car	Vampire
Needle	Rock	Spotlight	Videotape
Nose	Rocket	Square	Vulture
Onion	Roof	Staircase	Water
Pants	Room	Star	Weapon
Parachute	Rope	Stomach	Web
Passport	Rust	Sun	Weed
Pebble	Saddle	Sunglasses	Wheelchair
Pencil	Salt	Swimming pool	Window
Pendulum	Sandpaper	Sword	Woman
Pepper	Sandwich	Table	Worm
Perfume	Satellite	Tapestry	X-ray

12 Manipulative Verbs

Context

Many idea-generation techniques focus on the creation of something new, novel or innovative – helping to get the ball rolling, so to speak. However, a creative block can easily occur later in the process, when we have chosen a suitable idea, yet are unable to articulate it in an appropriate way. In these moments, we can feel stuck, not knowing what to do next, having exhausted any immediate options. We may even begin to doubt the original idea – taking us right back to square one. We all find ourselves in this situation from time to time, thinking that our concepts are perhaps a little on the safe side, or maybe reflecting on existing ideas too closely. In these moments, stepping back and reimagining the subject of study can help.

As we mention in Random Nouns (pp. 134–139), the fundamental binary division for virtually every natural language is that of nouns (things) vs verbs (actions). So, if you're unhappy with the *thing* you have created, or it's not working in the way you wish, one response could be to apply an *action* to it.

'Reimagine your subject by applying a series of verbs to it. Performing actions such as multiply, divide, invert, transpose, freeze, flatten, soften, or extrude can allow designers to quickly generate diverse solutions to a problem.'

Don Koberg [12]

Helps: Move from being stuck to unstuck when developing ideas.

Time: 1–2 hours+.

Tools: Pencil, paper, sticky notes.

Practice: Take a thing. Apply an action.

1 | Take one of your ideas (this could be a visual solution you created from the Random Nouns exercise or something from a current project).

2 | Choose a Manipulative Verb (from the Manipulative Verbs list on pp. 142–143).

3 | Apply the verb to your idea and see what effect this action has.

4 | How does the verb change the idea?

5 | Create a visual response as quickly as you can.

6 | Repeat this exercise with different Manipulative Verbs.

7 | Document what happens. Reflect on which verbs worked well for you.

Abstract	Dissect
Adapt	Divide
Add	Eliminate
Alter	Enrich
Amend	Exclude
Attract	Expand
Combine	Expose
Compare	Flatten
Compliment	Freeze
Compress	Gather
Conform	Germinate
Criticize	Harden
Darken	Include
Dilute	Integrate

Invert	Reverse
Join	Rotate
Joke	Separate
Lighten	Soften
Loosen	Squeeze
Magnify	Stretch
Minimize	Subdue
Modify	Substitute
Multiply	Subtract
Organize	Symbolize
Protect	Thicken
Rearrange	Transpose
Repeat	Unite
Repel	Widen

13 The Power of Reading

Context

Helps: Explore in and around an existing idea to develop its potential.

Time: 1–2 hours+.

Tools: Pencil, paper, sticky notes.

The Latin *legere* means not only 'to read', but also 'to choose', or 'to select'.

Reading is an autobiographical, anonymous and generative act; the reader essentially creates a visual aesthetic of the work. We never really understand the writer's intention because each time we read a book, we make it our own. We seem to find, in book after book, the tales of our own lives. 'To write down one's impression of *Hamlet* as one reads it year after year,' wrote Virginia Woolf, 'would be virtually to record one's own autobiography.'[13]

The autobiographical nature of reading, what we bring to the experience, and how there can never be just one reading of a piece of work, is incredibly compelling. Readers come prepared (consciously or otherwise) to make a narrative interpretation of any given text, and it's always their responsibility to attribute that meaning as part of the encounter. When we read, we tend to find our own identity as themes within the text using the work of others to symbolize and embody ourselves. ('Our memory, like our minds, is reductive ... we are constantly selecting and reducing' – Jean-Claude Carrière.[14])

Reading is, therefore, a *generative* act. So, can we use it to *generate* ideas?

In this exercise, we repeat the process from Random Nouns (pp. 134–139), but this time using a full page from any novel, newspaper or textbook.

Practice (Select and reduce)

1 | Choose a subject (or question, or define a problem) for which you wish to generate ideas.

2 | Grab any book/magazine/newspaper and select one page at random.

3 | Now, select 10 words from the text and arrange them in order of importance. You decide what you think has value; you only need to justify your choices to yourself (there are no right answers).

4 | With each of your selected words in turn, walk towards your subject (or question, or problem). Attempt to form connections between the word and the subject. Generate as many ideas as possible in response to your 10 words.

5 | Next, evaluate the page of text as a whole. How do you feel about it? Write this down as a simple proposition. Use the statement as raw material and attempt to form a connection between it and your subject. Again, try to generate as many ideas as possible.

We have run this workshop with individuals and groups, using random pages taken from a tabloid newspaper, an arts manifesto, a semiotics essay, a celebrity chef cookbook, a trashy romance novel... Any text can serve as useful raw material to translate into ideas.

Reflect

- Which text was best for generating ideas?
- How do you feel about the ideas you've generated?
- What type of words were useful to you in this exercise: nouns/verbs/adjectives?
- Which were not?
- Compile your own top 10 most fruitful words.
- Create an ever-growing list of words that tend to work for you, which can become a simple but useful toolkit for future idea generation.

Text Types

Tabloid newspaper
Arts manifesto
Semiotics essay
Celebrity chef cookbook
Trashy romance novel
Graphic novel
True-crime book
Computer magazine
Historical fiction
Autobiography
Prayer book
Memoir
Poetry
Travel guide
Self-help manual
Classic play scripts
Personal diary
Political thriller
Paranormal romance
Encyclopedia

14 The 90-Minute Rule

Context

Work overload is just a distraction. The culture of the doer, the arrive early/leave late mentality isn't the recipe for success. It just suggests a lack of priority.

Few people genuinely pay attention to their bodies' natural rhythms, but if you do, you'll find we're all a little different in terms of what makes us tick. What unites us, however, is that our bodies operate on cycles called *ultradian rhythms*. Nathaniel Kleitman, a ground-breaking sleep researcher, identified the *basic rest–activity cycle* – the 90-minute periods during which you progress through the five stages of sleep.[15] These patterns can also be found in our waking hours, as we move from higher to lower alertness. During these cycles, there's a point when we're most energized and a period when we're fatigued. Our energy reserves diminish as the day wears on, which is why you're most active in the morning.

Your brain can only maintain a focus for limited periods of time, as it burns through most of its glucose (the sugar responsible for optimal brain function) in approximately 90-minute intervals. After this period, if you take short scheduled breaks of 20 to 30 minutes, it can allow the brain to rebuild its store of glucose. This renews the energy needed, both physically and mentally, to prepare you for another 90 minutes of activity. Doing this can help you get things done in a third of the time it would usually take.

Practice

This leads us to the 90-Minute Rule. There are many versions of this, and people have been asserting their versions for many years. The basic principle is:

- *focus (90 minutes)*
- *then rest (20–30 minutes)*

Helps: Utilize time more efficiently and reduce creative fatigue.

Time: 2-hour bursts.

Tools: Whatever you're currently working with.

It's as simple as that.

Focus.

Then rest.

Our self-control is like a muscle, and the longer the day goes on, the more fatigue sets in. Hence the advice to carry out your most significant tasks first thing in the morning. Try to eliminate distractions from this 90-minute block. Responding to text messages or emails can hijack your focus and put you in a reactive mode, so try to remove these entirely. Resist the *pull* of the *push* notification.

It's also important to remember the human element in our work, practice and creative pursuits. The time we spend resting is just as (if not more) important than the time we spend focusing. Planning our rest time (walking, daydreaming, etc.) needs to be built into our work planning.

- Get a diary.
- Actively include rest time in your working day, in and around dedicated tasks (initially using the 90-Minute Rule).
- Reflect on and adjust the timings once you've seen it work (or not) in practice.

Reflect

Another iteration of this idea worth exploring is the *Pomodoro Technique*, developed by Francesco Cirillo, which works on a 25-minute (focus), 5-minute (rest) cycle, with a longer break every four cycles.[16] A further example is the Unschedule, developed by psychologist Neil Fiore and detailed in his book *The Now Habit*.[17] What's important to remember with all of these methods, though, is that everyone is different; the key lies in finding out when, where and how your own version of the focus/rest balance works best.

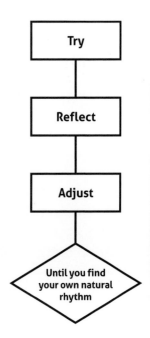

15 Murakami day
(Write—Run—Relax)

Helps: Embrace a radically different working practice.

Time: 1 day+.

Tools: Writing pen, lined paper, shoes to run in, a good novel, some great music.

Context

This exercise is another example of the Library Book Persona exercise on pp. 106–111 (see also Goldsworthy Day on pp. 188–193). It's simple to do, and it's great for introducing a more radical shift in your normal working practice – this has certainly been true for us and our students. Many do it just once, and integrate a few references into their own practice. Others end up re-engineering their entire craft in the light of their discoveries, and adopting many of Murakami's habits as their own.

For this writing challenge, simply adopt Haruki Murakami's routine for a day.

'When I'm in writing mode for a novel, I get up at four a.m. and work for five to six hours. In the afternoon, I run for ten kilometers or swim for fifteen hundred meters (or do both), then I read a bit and listen to some music. I go to bed at nine p.m.'

Haruki Murakami [18]

Practice: Timescales

4 am: Wake up. Then start writing.

10 am: Stop writing.

12 pm: Take a 10k run or 1,500m swim (or both).

3 pm: Enjoy a relaxing afternoon; read a novel, listen to music.

9 pm: Go to bed.

the more I write,
the more I like
everything

* Write from memory.
* Don't edit anything, just write.
* Write using a fountain pen on lingled paper

Practice: Context

'As I wrote *A Wild Sheep Chase*, I came to feel strongly that a story, a *monogatari*, is not something you create. It is something that you pull out of yourself. The story is already there, inside you. You can't make it, you can only bring it out. This is true for me, at least: it is the story's spontaneity. For me, a story is a vehicle that takes the reader somewhere. Whatever information you may try to convey, whatever you may try to open the reader's emotions to, the first thing you have to do is get that reader into the vehicle. And the vehicle – the story – the *monogatari* – must have the power to make people believe. These above all are the conditions that a story must fulfill.'

Haruki Murakami [19]

Practice: Rules

- Write from memory.
- Don't edit anything, just write.
- Write using a fountain pen on lined paper.

'When I began writing *A Wild Sheep Chase* I had no preset program in mind. I wrote the opening chapter almost at random. I still had absolutely no idea how the story would develop from that point. But I experienced no anxiety, because I felt – I knew – that the story was there, inside me. I was like a dowser searching for water with his divining rod. I knew – I felt – that the water was there. And so I started to dig.'

Haruki Murakami [19]

16 Play (Games)

Context

Ordinary parlour games can help you develop the valuable skill of coupling *ideas* with *craft* – forcing you to engage in quick-response idea generation, and then to communicate your ideas with clarity through verbal, written or visual forms. Workshops in these core skills, not surprisingly, already exist in the form of three games: Pictionary, Articulate and Squint.

Pictionary: where you have to communicate a word to your team via *drawing* only.

Articulate: where you have to communicate a word to your team *verbally* without mentioning it explicitly.

Squint: similar to Pictionary, where you have to communicate a word to your team using only pre-existing geometric shapes.

A relaxed and playful atmosphere helps to reduce the pressure-induced anxiety we may associate with idea generation. Once we recognize the connection between the play and the ease in which we come up with new ideas during a game, we can then deliberately and intentionally introduce a more playful approach to our creative processes.

A critical aspect of our play is the solving of a puzzle. We take great pleasure in pattern-finding, and the challenge

Helps: Translate literal game play into creative play.

Time: 1–4 hours+.

Tools: Pencil, paper, a board game: Pictionary, Articulate or Squint.

'Play is also about being present in life, loving life, exploring life and rejoicing in life.'

Ann Charlotte Thorsted [20]

of seeking out the right answer is something many of us rise to. If the connection fits, then it brings us a sense of satisfaction. This is another example of the habit loop in action: cue, routine, reward (see Chapter 2, p. 42) – the benefit here being that the game play encourages our minds to stay poised, ready to respond, and we can replicate this in our wider creative practice.

Practice

Version 1: Collaborative play
1 | Play Pictionary, Articulate and/or Squint in a group for 30 minutes.

2 | Consider afterwards:
• Your feelings (especially anxiety) at the beginning/middle/end of the game.
• The fluency of your thinking towards the end of the game.
• How does developing ideas within a game differ from your normal practice?
• What can you integrate into your normal practice?

Version 2: Integration
1 | Use the game cards as triggers for idea generation (in response to a project brief you are working on).

2 | Respond to any thought/idea, via:
• drawing only
• verbally without mentioning it specifically
• composing it using only pre-existing shapes

3 | Reflect on the experience using the same questions asked for Version 1.
• Consider your feelings (especially anxiety) at the beginning/middle/end of the activity.
• Describe the fluency of your thinking towards the end of the process.
• How does developing ideas this way differ from your normal practice?
• What can you integrate into your evolving way of working?

17 Passive/Active

Helps: Quieten the noise of the moment and to think clearly.

Time: 2–3 hours+.

Tools: Voice recorder (smartphone or similar).

Context

Creative practice is known for its immersive nature – we rarely switch off, and ideas can come at any moment. Without deliberate *passive* spaces in between the focused *active* thinking and making, there's a real danger that the constant noise of productivity will become too much for us to make any sense of it all. Both need to be given appropriate, deliberate space to contribute to the whole that is your creativity.

Passive and active.
Breathe in. Breathe out.

This will, of course, mean different things to different people, and the balance will invariably change across the course of an individual project or career. For many, that space is nature. Or the focused immersion that comes when listening to music attentively (rather than as a soundtrack to another activity). Or the quiet rhythms that emerge out on a run, a ride or a swim. There are many versions and you will have (or will find) yours.

Practice

So, at the moment in time when you are more aware of the noise around you, when the ideas have stopped flowing, or when you can no longer see the wood for the trees:

- Stop and go *out* for 2 to 3 hours.
- Go on your own.
- Carry a voice recorder (smartphone in flight mode, please).
- Leave the pressure of your day/week *out there* somewhere.
- Don't consciously focus on the work itself; connect to that moment – mindful of your breathing, the ground under your feet, sounds around you. As thoughts, observations or ideas about your work/process float to the surface, record them verbally.

18 Format

Helps: Open up or refine new ways of recording our thinking.

Time: 1–3 hours+.

Tools: Pencil, paper, various physical and digital substrates.

Context

As with many of the factors that shape our capacity to grow creatively, God (or is it the Devil?) is in the detail. Embracing the important underlying principles (identity, habit, play) is only part of the story. Learning to navigate the subtleties of our craft – particularly over time – is often where the magic lies, especially when it comes to the things we take for granted. The theory is all well and good (and always much neater than practice), but getting your hands dirty, embracing the unknown, or revisiting well-trodden paths afresh can offer alternative ways of looking at our practice.

Some of these practical explorations can seem so trivial or obvious that we routinely ignore them – thinking them irrelevant to the issues at large. As our careers develop, the challenge becomes less about tackling any given activity in and of itself, and more about overcoming any mindset that suggests trying something new is likely to be a waste of time.

Practice

Format (and by this, we mean the tangible form by which you capture your creative thinking) is, from our experience, one of those considerations that on the surface seems likely to have little impact on your overall creativity. A good idea is a good idea regardless of how or where it's recorded. However, whatever your personal preference is for recording your thoughts, we're also interested in the way in which our capturing those ideas can condition, limit or enhance how you work. A large, blank page can be intimidating for some, yet can invite lots of iterative expressions of the same idea, helping it evolve. Bound pages are great for keeping your thoughts together, but tend to lock ideas into a linear record, burying great ideas in a mountain of thinking.

Part 1

Rather than tell you what format to use (we are all different, and projects demand different tools), we'd like to encourage you to consider how a variety of formats can open up or close down your thinking and the development of ideas. Using the suggestion below, create an evolving list of the positive/negative opportunities offered by each format – starting with a general overview, and then looking specifically at each format in the context of three recent projects. Try to go beyond the immediate, and consider the details. We've listed a few standard formats, but add others that relate to your discipline.

Format	+ (positive)	
Scale (large)		
Scale (medium)		
Scale (small)		
Bound sheets (sketchbooks)		
Loose sheets (layout)		
Sticky notes		
Physical		
Digital		
Audio (speech)		
Temporary (pencil)		
Permanent (pen)		
Other#1		
Other#2		
Other#3		

Part 2

Actively explore more radical/experimental/contextual formats and processes to record ideas – particularly those less common in your normal discipline. Add to the matrix as you try new methods, recording the + / – / ? attributes accordingly. Consider factors such as:

- Scale (go significantly beyond what is comfortable or practical).
- Temporary/permanent (create rules that destroy/preserve your work).
- How does this change your engagement with the act of recording?
- Time (the speed in which you document your ideas).
- Fluency (the ease with which you can record your ideas).

– (negative)	? (when to use)

19 Flattery is a Compliment

Helps: Utilize copying as a springboard for new ideas.

—————

Time: 1–8 hours+.

—————

Tools: Pencil, paper, various creative tools (camera, computer, etc.), existing artworks.

—————

Context

While creativity has much to do with the self-expression of the individual, this rarely happens in isolation. Even if you work on your own, you're invariably communicating with someone through whatever it is you make. We might collaborate with others face to face in an office or studio, or remotely online – and this may even happen indirectly through a detached combination of our respective crafts, rather than a shared discussion around our ideas. We may also create work that has a connection to the work of others, either directly or indirectly.

Inevitably, collaboration involves communication, cooperation and compromise, which all centre on how we relate to and act with other people. Working with others happens best when people feel comfortable together, and you'll be familiar with the process of sharing thoughts and ideas through some form of ice-breaker (especially with new teams). *Play*, as a mode of thinking and interaction, can perform a critical role in helping provide a space where ideas are supported and encouraged by others.

Ultimately, above and beyond all of these attributes, one of the most positive things about collaboration is the opportunity it provides us to learn from others. If we are working alone, we can still learn from others through analysing how they operate (see Library Book Persona, pp. 106–111). We can also learn much from past masters by copying their work. Hunter S. Thompson, on more than one occasion, typed out the entire manuscript of *The Great Gatsby* to feel what it was like to write a masterpiece. Ernest Hemingway also recommended this approach (only for shorter passages) to practise writing from the perspective of another writer.

Within our work, we should attempt to remain open and to embrace new experiences. Doing so enables us to reflect on our subsequent responses and, where appropriate, to integrate these into our evolving practice. Try the following exercises (in any order), which explore notions of cooperation, collaboration and copying as a means of creative growth.

Practice

Workshop: Gesture
Here is an adaptation of a classic improv game (we're unsure of its exact origins).

- Everyone stands in a circle.
- Person A makes a small gesture.
- The person beside them repeats the gesture, and so on around the ring.

The point of the exercise is to keep the gesture exactly the same. Everyone has to concentrate and pay attention to the action so as to repeat it correctly (it's harder to do than you think). You can also do the same exercise but with sounds instead of gestures (and there are multiple versions of this activity, often used within the performing arts). These exercises are useful, not just in terms of breaking the ice and encouraging communication within new teams, but also in helping develop our ability to observe and focus. We appreciate this type of activity is not to everyone's taste, so try it out if you're curious, and skip it if not. The main reason for its inclusion here is to highlight its underlying principles (imitation, duplication and repetition), which all feature in the following two activities, too.

Workshop: At a distance
This exercise also works well remotely with your chosen discipline: photography, drawing, music, etc., via email or post.

1 | Person A makes a photograph/drawing/piece of music and sends it to person B.

'If you type out somebody's work, you learn a lot about it. Amazingly it's like music. And from typing out parts of Faulkner, Hemingway, Fitzgerald – these were writers that were very big in my life and the lives of the people around me – so yeah I wanted to learn from the best I guess.'

Hunter S. Thompson [21]

2 | Person B recreates the piece from scratch as accurately as possible and sends it to Person C, and so on around the circle of collaborators.

3 | Finally, exhibit all the outcomes in one place (physical or digital).

Workshop: Listen to Agnes

'You must discover the artwork that you like and realize the response you make to it. You must especially know the response you make to your own work. It is in this way that you discover your own direction and the truth about yourself.'

Agnes Martin[22]

1 | Select an artwork you admire.
Ask yourself how the work makes you feel?

2 | Attempt to recreate the work as precisely as possible.
Ask yourself how the recreation of the work makes you feel?

3 | Create a response to the original work in any medium.
Ask yourself how your response to the work makes you feel?

Workshop: Grids, by Jocelyn Affleck

Start by drawing a row of 30 squares horizontally on a sheet of paper. Try to keep these as uniform as possible. Then, pass the sheet to another person and ask them to copy the row of 30 squares, creating a new row underneath.

Repeat this 30 times. The more people involved in the experiment, the more diverse the results will be.

Right: Grids by Jocelyn Affleck

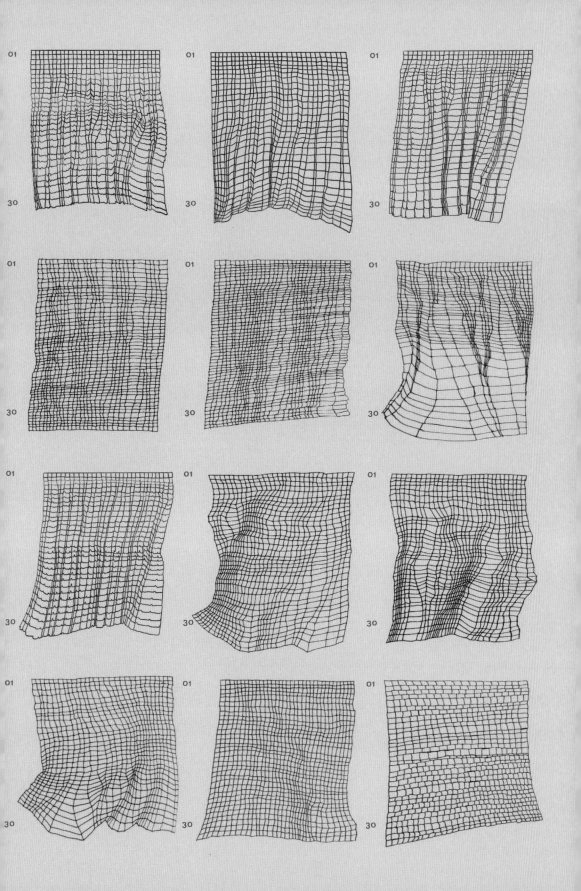

20 Atelier

Context

There are many ways of *being* in the world. The environment, conditions and structures (both physical and cultural) within which we operate can shape us creatively in various ways. Often these effects may not be immediately noticeable – however, when we make dramatic changes to our environment or the structure of our daily lives, they can come into sharp focus. As a simple example of this, consider how your moods, behaviours and actions change when you are on holiday.

Creativity is a combination of structure and chance, a constant challenge to the status quo. What if we view our whole lives more creatively, and consciously adjust any dull or mundane aspects of our daily routine? In particular, how would things improve if we asked ourselves: 'How can I tweak/amend/adjust/change the structure of my environment?'

As an illustration of this, when Dion thinks or writes, he needs to immerse himself in quiet solitude. However, once he's working up an idea, he finds it much more comfortable if he listens to music. When making logical choices, he needs to hear his thoughts and will often talk through his ideas with others. Merely discussing them out loud makes him more decisive about which direction to take. Similarly, some of us may naturally feel alive in the mornings, while for others, it will be later at night.

Practice

Start with your immediate environment, and ask yourself what might happen if you worked in a different space? What spaces do you have access to? Can you identify which areas allow you to be the most creative, productive, decisive, bold, free? We'll naturally find that some spaces are more comfortable for concentration, while others are better for the generation of new ideas.

Helps: Define the spaces you work in as creative assets.

Time: 2–8 hours+.

Tools: Pencil, paper, camera, access to a variety of spaces or environments.

What is the environment in which you work best? As a simple exercise, try to work in a different space for at least an hour each day and analyse the effect the environment has on your thoughts and ideas (and see also Goldsworthy Day on pp. 188–193, and Murakami Day on pp. 148–151). The following is a specific application of this thinking that we've used with students:

Atelier (A)

1 | Photograph your current workspace.

2 | Spend 10 minutes considering its qualities and list the essential elements (there may not be many).

3 | Ask yourself: 'Why is this the right place for my practice?'

Atelier (B)

1 | Consider your current working environment in relation to the particular actions relevant to your practice (research, idea generation, drawing, making, writing, etc.). Create a list and then decide on what you feel are the three main activities.

2 | What would be the ideal set-up for these individual activities? How would each space look? Write or sketch your thoughts. You may find that one area would be perfect for all, or you may need to design a unique space for each separate activity.

3 | In your immediate vicinity, what other alternative spaces are available to you? Identify three areas within your home/place of work where you could create your new set-up. Try each one out, then reflect on the effect each environment has on your thoughts and ideas.

4 | Photograph each of these spaces.

Atelier al fresco

1 | Identify the nearest outdoor space where you could duplicate this new set-up, with minimal fuss and without altering the proportions of your working area.

2 | Then, try it out (consider this a temporary, or 'pop-up', workspace).

3 | Photograph your *atelier al fresco* workspace.

Atelier nouveau

The nature of our daily practice means that what we do, and the environment we do it in, becomes habitual. As a result, we rarely question it. Through pushing back at your habits – and in this case, the space you operate in – you can discover which aspects of your environment are working with you or against you. Next, embrace the notion of *play* and try to push the limits of what is possible.

1 | Create yourself a temporary work area (a studio space ripe for play) in one (or all) of the following types of spaces: open, enclosed, quiet, loud, indoor, outdoor, natural, man-made, small, large, dark, bright, shared, isolated, warm, cold…

2 | Photograph your *atelier nouveau* workspace.

Reflect

Collate all of your atelier workspace photographs and put them somewhere prominent for a few weeks. Reflect on them each time your creativity or productivity slows, and respond accordingly.

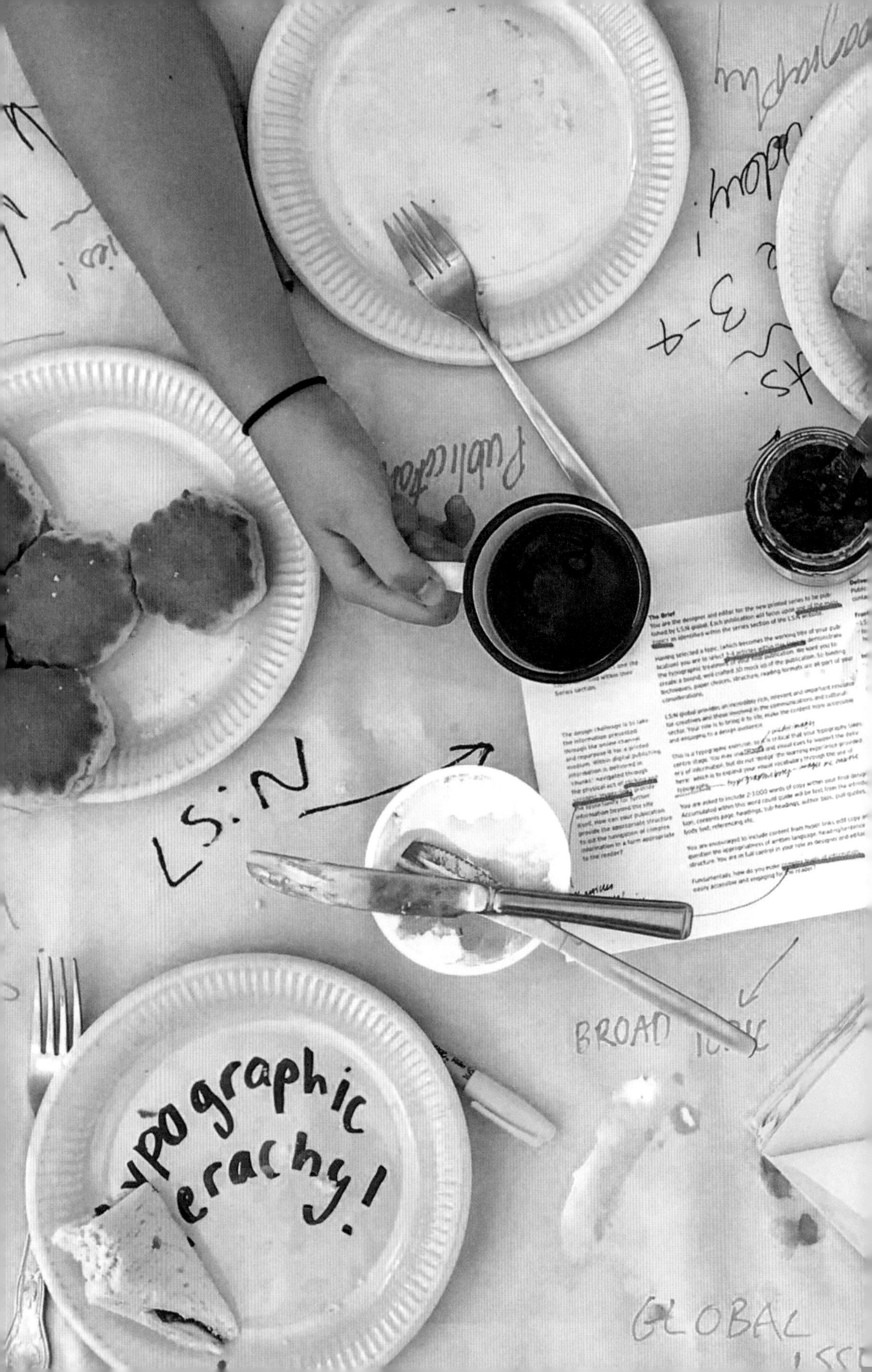

LS:N
BROAD
ypographic
erachy!
GLOBAL

21 Scottish Plumber
(from Phil Carter)

Helps: Build creative connections between disparate themes.

———————————

Time: 1 hour+.

———————————

Tools: Pencil, paper, sticky notes.

———————————

Context

Phil tells of a project he worked on for the human resources department of the London Underground – essentially letting the employees know that this was *their* HR. The process he used illustrates an exercise that has helped countless students.

> **'On most projects, I still go straight to the sketch pad and start putting down thoughts – often as lists or doodles, as it helps me to clear my head.'**
>
> Phil Carter [23]

'There's the classic Tube sign, the stations, the colours, escalators, tickets, and I'll write them all down as a long list as quickly as possible. After a while, it will come down to a top five of the key things that say 'London Underground' – or whatever the subject is. Then I'll make a second list and I'm thinking, 'Okay, so HR is really about people. What things best capture people?', so you go through all of those and record them alongside the first. All the time you're looking for a thread, a spark that might connect the two. Most of the time there is no thread, but you never really know unless you try.'

Practice

This exercise is great at the beginning of a project. You only need to spend 20 to 30 minutes, and you can return to it as your understanding of the subject (and its possibilities) grows.

Part 1 *10–15 minutes*
1 | Write down the key themes that relate to your project.

2 | Pick 2 that feel the most pertinent (perhaps one specific and one generic) and use these as your headings, or themes.

3 | Add as many relevant words under each theme as possible.

Part 2 *10–15 minutes*
1 | Look for immediate connections between the two lists. Where are the possible sparks? Start by identifying any similar words or themes.

2 | Identify a top 5 for each (that express each theme succinctly).

3 | Move on to forcing words together as random collisions to see what you find. Write and/or draw any possible connections (no matter how tenuous).

4 | Keep going for as long as you have the energy, but don't exhaust yourself (it's just a warm-up).

5 | When you feel you've identified as many connections as you can, move on to developing some of the emerging ideas further.

'So, you're a Scottish plumber. You need an identity. What could it be? We were always coming up with the Loch Ness monster with huge bends, and it got your brain thinking.'

Phil Carter [23]

This page: From a sketchbook by Phil Carter

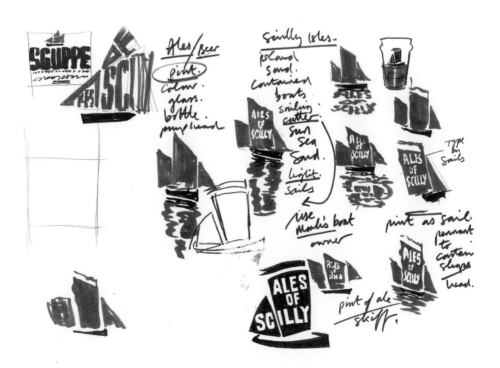

22 Visual Volume

Context

Helps: Refine and develop existing ideas mid-project.

Time: 1–8 hours+.

Tools: Marker, masking tape, pencil and paper.

This is a useful perspective to embrace when you have a few evolving ideas, but are beginning to feel like you're going around in circles trying to move them forward. The principles behind it can work at any stage of a process and are built on the notion of translating practices across disciplines.

Music, and particularly the process of writing and recording a song, carries many parallels that can be re-appropriated in the visual world (and vice versa). Historically, at the beginning of a recording project, a sound engineer would run a line of masking tape along the front edge of the mixing desk, labelling each channel with the corresponding instrument (kick drum, snare drum, lead vocal, etc.). Once everything was recorded – either all together (live), or instrument by instrument (tracked) – the individual elements would be mixed so that they complemented each other.

The mixing process is at the core of song development. A good mix can elevate disparate elements into a unified whole that far exceeds a song's initial potential. A bad mix can leave a song dead in the water. Mixing essentially considers each element in relation to the next, and to the song as a whole – seeking an appropriate balance that pulls the best characteristics together. A mix is ultimately a creative perspective, and (importantly) there is more than one good version (hence the proliferation of remixes in popular music).

The metaphor of a *visual* (rather than audio) mixing desk is pretty straightforward, and most of us are using it intuitively at some level when we create anything new. Embracing it deliberately, however, is a valuable mechanism to help move beyond moments of developmental block. We tend to get to a point where all the right visual elements are in place (colours, materials, images, etc.) but the mix is wrong. The problem here is that we can become progressively entrenched in a particular expression of an idea – trying to make it work, and in doing so, increasingly shutting out any alternative ways of arranging things. By intentionally remixing what is there, and repeating this action several times, we generate iterative adaptations of the same idea. We're still using the same building blocks, but are becoming less precious with our work – more open to alternatives. This exercise helps to clarify what's ultimately central and what's peripheral. Even if you then return to your original version, you do so with far greater confidence in each constituent part, and any underlying communication tends to be clearer as a result.

Practice

Consider the individual elements of a piece of visual work as if they were channels on a mixing desk, systematically adjusting each one in turn to see how the change affects the whole.

- Run a line of masking tape across a table/sketchbook/etc.
- List all the components of your <insert current project>.
- Systematically adjust each one in your work and record the impact.
- Focus on one component at a time to begin with.
- Progress to changing multiple components concurrently.
- Remove some elements entirely.
- Think about visual effects: scale, repetition, layers, spatial relationship, etc.
- Is anything too loud?
- What is fighting for space?
- Saturate.
- Desaturate.
- Quieter.
- Louder.
- Depth of field?
- Materials?
- Physical size?
- And so on.

| CONTEXT | ECONOMY | SPEED | HANDLING | FLEXIB- -ILITY | SAFETY | E... |

| PAGE SIZE | STOCK | MARGINS | DISPLAY TYPE | TEXT TYPE | TYPE SIZES | I... |

| LOGO | NAVIGATION | BG IMAGE | MAIN COPY | INTRO TXT | IMG SEQUEN... |

| SECURITY | MATERIALS | QUALITY | H&S | COST | AESTHE... |

| ANATOMY | FUNCTION | USE | MATERIALS | STRUCTURE | STYLE |

| SPIRIT | LEGIBLE | READ- ABLE | STYLE | STROKE | CONTRAST | |

POWER | SIZE | WEIGHT | AIRFLOW | COMFORT | COST |

EGATIVE SPACE | LINE FEED | JUSTIF--ICATION | PHOTO CREDITS | PAGE # | GUTTER |

TES |

ITY | FORM | CULTURE | TOUCH | COHESION | SPACE | DURA--BILITY |

T | FLEX | SOLE | STITCH | WEIGHT | BALANCE | GAIT |

| GLUES | SUPPORT |

VERSA--TILITY | STRES | BIAS | F | | COUNTERS | CURVES | STEMS |

23 Child's Play

Context

Much of the extensive research that's been done into play focuses on the many positive effects it has on the developing brain of a child. However, the research also states that it's vital for adults, too. We just don't see play as an *adult* thing, yet we're advised to engage in some sort of *body*, *object* and *social* play on a regular basis to avoid burnout and stress.

Body play: Active movement with no time or outcome pressures.

Object play: Creating something (anything) using your hands.

Social play: Purposeless social activities (talking about the weather or taking part in a pub quiz).

Ultimately, it doesn't matter which of these you spend your time on, so long as you play.

Gordon M. Burghardt, an evolutionary biologist at the University of Tennessee, describes how the happiness and renewed energy you'll experience from playing will 'more than compensate for the time "lost".'[24] In the novella *Naïve. Super* by Erlend Loe, the protagonist, struggling with his place in the world, decides to return to something he felt he understood – the simple act of bouncing a ball.[25] He remembers that when bouncing a ball as a child, he was happy. So, to reconnect with this sense of happiness, he returns to that activity. Later, he moves on to something better suited to confined spaces – a small hammer-and-shapes toy, which offers him a similar nostalgic connection with greater convenience. During this play (which sometimes lasts a whole day!) he finds a way to remember who he was.

What does it mean for an adult to spend the best part of a day bouncing a ball? (Indeed, what does it mean for the authors writing this down and suggesting it to others in print?)

Helps: Reconnect with child-like play as a creative release.

Time: 1–4 hours+.

Tools: Objects or spaces that facilitate your own version of child-like play.

Right: 94.7 Cycle Challenge (2006, image by Juliana Smith). South African performance artist Anthea Moys's work plays with the accepted 'rules of play', playfully challenging us to rethink rules we abide by.

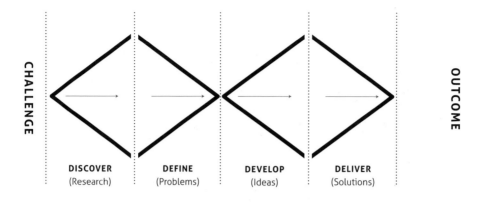

Fig.1: Original Design Council Double Diamond

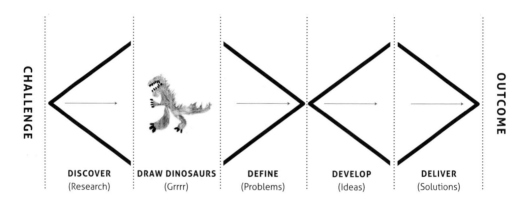

Fig.2: Enhanced 'Dinosaur' Double Diamond

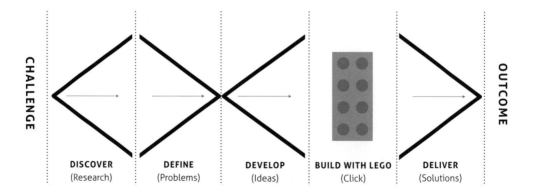

Fig.3: Enhanced 'Lego Brick' Double Diamond

As a child, you may – like us – have loved simply making things with your hands, or dismantling and reconstructing household objects, or drawing all day (or even bouncing balls). Why not, as an adult, continue to do so simply for fun, happiness and renewed energy?

Practice

Think back to when you were a child. What did you enjoy doing? Can you even remember? Try to reconnect with your childhood play and reimagine it as an activity you could do now.

Experiment 1

Decide what play activity you wish to recreate and then embed it as a critical (timetabled) part of your day/week/month.

Experiment 2

Embed your child's play so that it becomes a crucial part of your creative process, ready for when you next tackle a project. For example, the Design Council's classic Double Diamond process diagram[26] (a model developed after an extensive review of the working practice of many design agencies, that breaks a project down into four distinct creative phases: Discover, Define, Develop, Deliver) could become:

Discover, *Draw dinosaurs,* Define, Develop, Deliver.

Or

Discover, Define, Develop, *Build with Lego,* Deliver.

Visualize your own version as a physical design and put it somewhere prominent.

Opposite: Playing with the classic Double Diamond process model

24 Goldsworthy Day

Helps: Embrace a radically different working practice.

Time: 1 day+.

Tools: Pencil, paper, camera and an outdoor space to explore and make in.

Context

This Practice chapter evolved from a deep interest in how other people work creatively, and the reality that we all (you included) have a unique way of working from which others can learn. These observations naturally offer fresh perspectives when we hit any creative block (and we *all* do). 'Adopting a Persona' has become a familiar phrase in our conversations with students (and in our own practice) whenever we need to step sideways or recognize the value of a fresh approach.

Practice

The following is a simple outline that will frame a day of your time, based (loosely) on the working practice of UK artist Andy Goldsworthy. It's particularly relevant to those of us who spend more of our working day indoors rather than outdoors. Interpret the instructions as you see fit. You may also wish to complement these by reading up on Goldsworthy beforehand, or perhaps watching a documentary on his work (*Rivers and Tides* is a good place to start[27]).

Instructions

1 | Just before sunrise, get up and go for a walk.

2 | Allow your awareness of the weather and the environment to guide your journey.

3 | Stop at a place you connect with (for whatever reason).

4 | Allow yourself some time to reflect on the nature of that connection.

5 | Write or draw some of those reflections.

6 | While in situ, create a work that responds to your feelings about that place.

7 | Document your findings.

8 | Just after dusk, reflect on the day, noting any points of tension or progress.

Rules
- Use only the materials you find on-site.
- Use only natural materials (nothing machined).
- Treat the space with reverence and respect.
- Leave the space better than you found it.
- Record your activities photographically (process and outcomes).

Evening reflections

- How did this day differ from your normal practice?
- What did you find hard?
- What did you find easy?
- What did you enjoy?
- Were there moments when you were genuinely lost in play?
- How in control did you feel?
- Is this good/bad?
- Thoughts surrounding *place, materials* or *processes*?
- Thoughts surrounding *making* vs *documenting*?
- Which aspects of the day should you retain?
- Which should you ignore?
- Things to amplify?
- Things to reduce?
- How could your normal practice evolve in the light of the day?

'Mistakes are as important as successes.'

Andy Goldsworthy [28]

Page 189, opposite and following pages: Goldsworthy Day by Eleanor Smith, Draig Conybear and Dan Moggs

25 ProAm

Context

Our underlying attitude to the creative work we engage in and our sense of competency can have a significant bearing on our creativity. Self-belief, integrity and time-honoured ability, when harnessed well, can overcome significant challenges. Conversely, a lack of faith in these areas can have the opposite effect – incapacitating us, sometimes to the point of permanent inaction.

Our relationship to creative work begins as an amateur, perhaps with a keen interest in a discipline. Through practice, we may improve and eventually become an expert or professional in our field, but what do we mean by *professional*? Or *amateur*? Is one better than the other? Does someone become professional at whatever it is they do by completing a degree in the subject? Or is it when they're paid for their time? Is an amateur not qualified despite their ability? Or is engaging in an activity simply for the joy of it lost as soon as money enters the equation? You'll probably have your own sense of what validates either description.

The idea of the professional can suggest an authority on a subject matter. For those who desire to become a professional, this can also carry the need to have that authority. Conversely, many people are uncomfortable with the world of work, seeing their creative pursuits as a way to pull away from professionalism and the routines and conventions that go with it.

We have run several workshops that externalize our internal sense of creative worth, and how it plays a part in establishing significant behavioural change. The validation that comes with the tag *professional* is one way to gain confidence in what you're doing. Another is to question its authority, to confront its conventions and instead embrace the notion of the *amateur*.

Helps: Confront imposter syndrome or the need for creative validation.

Time: 1–8 hours+.

Tools: Pencil, paper, access to online printing suppliers, various materials.

I write for the joy of it.

'To be an amateur is to express the ancient French word: lover of, a person who engages for the pleasure of it. In many instances, amateurs are more competent than professionals, because they're more intimately connected to what they do. What they do is who they are.'

Andy Merrifield [29]

Practice

Part 1: Professional

Formally validating yourself as a professional is very easy to do. However, there's no quick fix to changing our internal view of self, and actually believing you are a professional can take time. Many people will still suffer from imposter syndrome even once they have a business card, years of experience or a collection of awards.

1 | Consider all the possible things you do/make/engage in and write a list of possible titles that describe these roles.

2 | Design a business card for each of these roles (yes, all of them) with your name, contact details and any other relevant information.

3 | Print your outcomes (ideally as actual business cards).

Part 2: Amateur

If you wish to avoid the limitations of the career path in favour of the life journey, then perhaps you'll find confidence in the following:

1 | Consider your craft, the things you do/make – your work – and write a list of possible actions that describe that work (write, make films, play the guitar, etc.):

I _____ for the pleasure of it.
Or, I _____ for the joy of it.
Or, I create _____ as quiet meditation.
And so on...

2 | Choose the best one (for whatever reason) and make an official sign/desk name/plaque that formally qualifies this belief.

Reflect

- Does seeing your name/role externalized change your sense of what you do?
- Are there any titles you're particularly proud of/excited about?
- Are there any that make you feel fraudulent?
- Why is this?
- Are there practical steps you can take to make any of them more likely?
- How does framing your craft in the light of *amateur* contrast to *professional*?
- Can you identify other individuals or ventures that embrace similar values?
- Where do you feel you sit in the tension between professional and amateur?

26 Translation

Context

We are all familiar with the idea of translation. A literal definition (courtesy of the *Oxford English Dictionary*) is 'the conversion of something from one form or medium into another'. English to Spanish. Solid to liquid. Theory to practice. And so on. Creatively, we should aim to develop both written records of our ideas (words, sentences, synonyms, etc.) *and* visual ones (pictures, sketches, storyboards, etc.). Reading the phrase 'an elephant juggling bicycles' will communicate a specific idea yet elicit a different visual image in the mind of every person who reads this book.[30] Capturing that difference is the heart of this principle.

Documenting the visual, however, is becoming less common as the arts are progressively marginalized in formal education. In addition, reading (words) and looking (pictures) use different collective parts of the brain (as does speaking), so expressing an idea solely as a piece of written text means we are only utilizing a limited percentage of our mind's computational power. It's like juggling with one hand tied behind your back – you can still do it, but you're exponentially more capable with two hands (and a trunk).

Helps: Systematically utilize more of your brain's creative power.

Time: 2–6 hours+.

Tools: Pencil, paper, development work for an old project, a podcast or interview.

Opposite: Sketchbook by Zach Rush

15

The notion of *creative translation* encourages taking an idea that exists in one form (the words *elephant, juggling* and/or *bicycles*) and systematically converting it into a visual language – often with multiple valid expressions. Once you start seeing the principle playing out in real time, every written note to self becomes a fertile well of possibility when trying to come up with new ideas. The discipline is in allowing yourself the time to do the hard work of converting the one to (potentially) many other expressions of the same idea.

Practice

Part 1: Current practice
Look back at the development work for a few of your recent projects:

- What percentage of your thinking is written or text vs drawn or image-based?
- Does this vary across the duration of the project?
- How does this alter from project to project?
- Conscious decision vs ingrained habit?

Part 2: Static translation
1 | Fold a large sheet of paper in half vertically (along the long side) to create 2 columns.

2 | Refer to the random nouns lists (pp. 136–139), and write the list vertically down the first column of your sheet.

3 | Translate each word into a visual sketch in the second column, allowing 10 seconds per word.

4 | Repeat this with an online image search for each word. Pick 3 images that express each word in a different way.

5 | Repeat this exercise using a newspaper article or a page from a novel, translating as many words as you can into drawn expressions.

Part 3: Dynamic translation

1 | Find a recorded conversation (podcast, interview, film dialogue, etc.).

2 | As you listen, capture as much of the discussion using drawings alone. (No writing allowed, except for names of people.) Spend at least 30 minutes doing this (and repeat it as a regular exercise).

3 | Return to your drawings later in the day and see what you can remember. Write some of the key themes down on a separate sheet.

4 | Translate these themes into images by making several online image searches, picking 3 images that express each theme in a different way.

5 | Repeat this exercise with a live conversation (overheard in a studio, bar, café, lecture, etc.).

Having observed this exercise in practice, we've noticed that individuals generally begin with a bias towards the written, and after a short period of dedicated adjustment, move to a more balanced split between written/visual recording. With persistence, some even manage to rewire their natural behaviour completely and form a new habit, regularly recording the majority of their thinking in the form of visual notes.

Reflect

Versatility is ultimately the key here, as different projects will require different processes. Reflect on the balance/relevance of the following for each project you undertake:
• Written
• Drawn
• Collage
• Spoken
• Photographed

'Creativity demands the ability to move back and forth between expansive thinking and close editing. Sketchbooks are an essential means by which designers catalogue their thoughts.'

Nancy Skolos and Thomas Wedell [31]

27 Random Objects

Helps: Introduce lateral thought into a project.

Time: 2–8 hours+.

Tools: Pencil, paper, an (evolving) collection of random objects.

Context

Rehearsing the process of connecting or re-combining existing elements is at the heart of much creative teaching. Part of the development of any project involves a period of research – gathering and editing elements so that connections can begin to be made and ideas can start to emerge. Similarly, those connections can come from anywhere and, for the practising artist or designer, sketchbooks are a place to gather material with long-term value. Looking back through old sketchbooks is often where lateral connections begin to appear because ideas come from more diverse reference points.

Practice

This exercise evolved from a brief focused on a very specific subject. Our students' thinking was tending to draw upon the same research themes, and their ideas were all looking a little similar. We needed to add a few conceptual curveballs into the mix, to try and encourage more lateral thinking in the emerging work. The following version of our resulting curveball is best done in a group, although it also works well individually.

'An idea is nothing more or less than a new combination of old elements ... consequently the habit of mind which leads to a search for relationships between facts becomes of the highest importance in the production of ideas.'

James Webb Young [32]

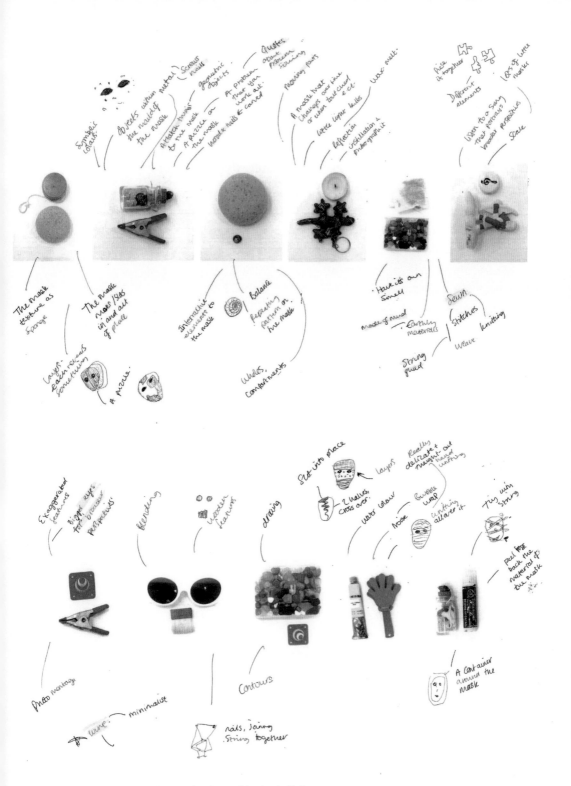

Above: Random Object collection (and notes) by Annie Haines

Part 1

Each person starts with an old shoebox (or similar).

1 | Fill the box with a collection of small, random (non-precious) objects.

2 | Aim for a wide variety of materials, shapes, sizes and colours.
The more you can collect, the more useful the exercise (25 minimum).

Part 2

1 | Arrange all the objects on a table (mix them up if you are working
as a group) and allow yourself a little time to appreciate the collection.

2 | Look for objects that resonate with you (for whatever reason).

3 | Assemble these to one side, but no more than 10 to 12 at a time.

4 | Take a photograph of them as an *edited* group.

5 | Then take a series of photographs of them in pairs or threes,
as seems fitting.

6 | Look for connections between the objects and record these as
quick sketches or sentences. The links could be physical (sharing
a shape, colour, material, or by being very different from each other),
or conceptual (representing similar or opposing ideas). The links could
be obvious, or abstract. Be open.

7 | Imagine stories that might come out of the relationship between
any given pair. Where are they from? Where could they be going?
What questions do they raise?

8 | Repeat the exercise and consider the individual objects (or groupings)
in the light of a current project (or themes within a project). How could
they influence your existing ideas? Could they lead to new ones?
Imagine the stories and questions this offers...

Reflect

As ever, ensure you record all of your thinking visually (as it occurs), and don't edit out ideas prematurely. We have seen the same individual use this exercise multiple times, with varying degrees of success – it tends not to be dependent on the individual, but rather on the project or context, so keep experimenting. As with the Mind Wandering (Jigsaw) exercise (pp. 130–133), this makes your (growing) collection of objects a useful long-term resource.

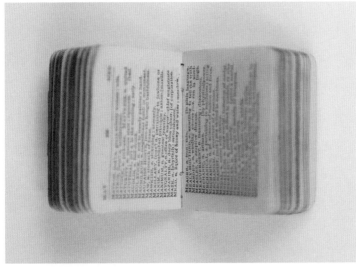

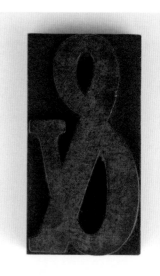
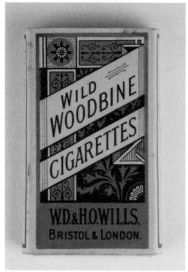

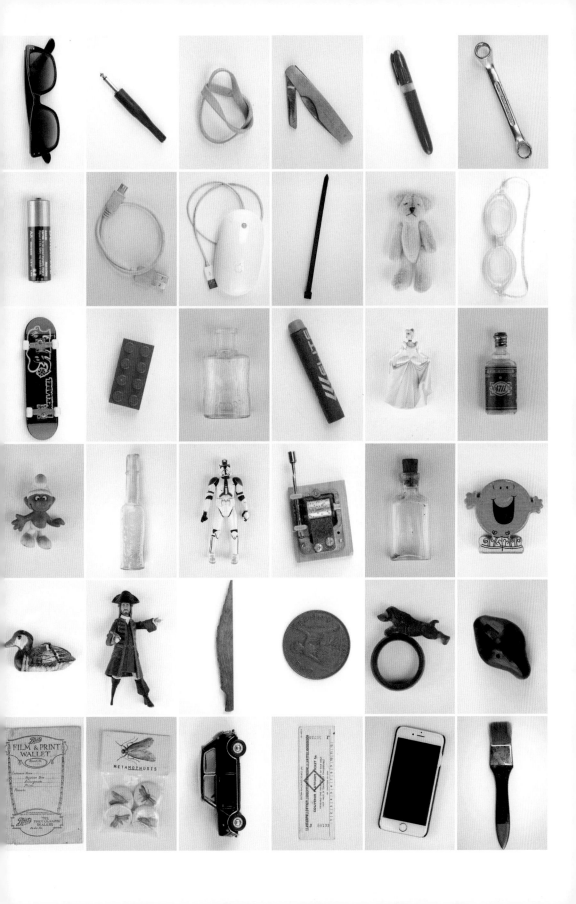

28 Play (Playmates)

Context

For much creative work developed in a commercial context, collaboration is vital – with people coming together in pursuit of a shared outcome. We need to be comfortable with our collaborators so that we can share our thoughts and ideas honestly with them. One sure-fire way to achieve this is through play, and the best way to enter a playful state is to throw off restraint through laughter and fun – often achieved through the playing of games. Humour makes us happy and is a massive contributor in the building and maintaining of relationships. Being able to *play along* is the first step to successful collaboration with others.

The following exercises use simple games as a way to break the ice, and set the scene for subsequent collaboration. You can use them as a way of helping people get to know one another, while simultaneously relaxing into a group environment. Play can act as a social leveller; formal hierarchies can be ignored in the context of a game.

Some of these activities can also make us laugh. And a working environment without laughter is unlikely to be as creative as one where it is present.

Practice

Step 1
Complete the Desire Lines exercise (pp. 122–125).

Step 2
1 | Email/call/write to each person in your People column with a list of themes from your Activities column that you're interested in exploring.

2 | Invite them to collaborate with you on a project and discuss the nature of the collaboration over a game of _____

Helps: Utilize collaborative play as a generative tool.

Time: 2–6 hours+.

Tools: Pencil, paper, a game to play, some collaborators.

(table tennis, Pictionary, online chess – whatever is relevant to you and the situation). The location could be drawn from your list of Places.

3 | Discuss your thoughts and ideas during the game.

4 | Conduct each subsequent meeting about your shared project through the playing of the game.

While there's no guarantee that your collaboration will be successful, the experience is at least likely to be playful and fun.

Reflect

In 2010, a study by Steven Johnson on the inventiveness of good commercial ideas revealed two critical insights: groups, rather than individuals, created two-thirds of successful inventions, and two-thirds were created without any explicit motive to make money.[33] This highlights the value of collaboration and all that it brings to creativity in terms of offering new perspectives and the chance to bounce ideas off others through social play and conversation. It also highlights the value in focusing on creativity for reasons other than the market (even if ultimately that may well be your goal).

'The creation of something new is not accomplished by the intellect but by the play instinct acting from inner necessity. The creative mind plays with the objects it loves.'

Carl Jung [34]

29 Combine

Context

Ideas are a new combination of known elements, and they are the result of unconscious recombination (by our artist selves). This essential collage exercise illustrates the simplicity of producing new ideas out of old ones.

Practice

Collage (from the French verb *coller*, meaning 'to glue') is the artistic process of gluing and assembling various materials to a flat surface. Collage can refer to both the actual procedure of cutting and pasting (the verb), as well as to the final artistic product (the noun).

1 | Select one of the word pairings listed opposite, or choose your own – perhaps linked to a current project or line of enquiry. Write down or draw your initial *literal* responses to each word in turn. Then, think of more *lateral* connections, and finally, consider *abstract* responses. You should end up with 2 lists and/or diagrams of literal-to-abstract associations, one for each word.

2 | Next, search for and select as many images as you can that you feel connect to or represent each of the 2 original words. Cut pictures out of old magazines, photographs, newspapers, ephemera, etc. Alternatively, you can source images online and print them out. Build on this by returning to your list of written/drawn responses from Step 1, and add to your growing collection of visual stimuli.

3 | Without thinking about it too much, quickly and simply play with (cut, tear, join, move, rearrange) the images in front of you and look for different visual combinations.

Helps: Embrace collage as a platform for idea generation.

Time: 2–6 hours+.

Tools: Pencil, paper, old magazines and newspapers, scissors, glue.

The collages in Chapters 1–3 were all created using this exercise – taking two random keywords from the surrounding texts (listed opposite) and generating ideas in response to them.

Sample word pairings

Dualism — Holism		Procrastination — Mathematics	
Suggest — Sublime		Measurement — Mental health	
Mystery — Perspective		Walk — Desk	
Balance — Distinctive		Artist — Guardian	
Manifesto — Control		Habit — Warrior	
Resistance — Enemy		Algorithm — Freedom	
Immune — Fears		Prize — Pretending	
Equation — Freefall		Improvisation — Adults	
Iterative — Nurturing		String — Reflex	
Connections — Surface		Risk — Education	
Curiosity — Muscle		Fun — Serious	
Cat — Loop		Activity — Exploration	
Premeditation — Block		Work — Play	
Craft — Life		Analogue — Intuition	
Structure — Chance		Happy — Curiosity	
Playing — Rules		Haydn — Lipstick	

4 | Create a new composition using your pool of gathered images that directly combines the 2 words. This could be as simple as making a combination with just 2 images, or it could be multiple images. Consider the composition, shape, colour and texture of your piece. You can communicate the words literally, laterally, subtly or loosely – any way you wish. Once you are happy with your composition, glue it down.

5 | Repeat for as many pairings as you have the energy. You may also wish to do an online image search for 'collage artist' for inspiration, between Steps 2 and 3.

'There is no such thing as a new idea. It is impossible. We simply take a lot of old ideas and put them into a sort of mental kaleidoscope. We give them a turn and they make new and curious combinations. We keep on turning and making new combinations indefinitely; but they are the same old pieces of colored glass that have been in use through all the ages.'

Mark Twain [35]

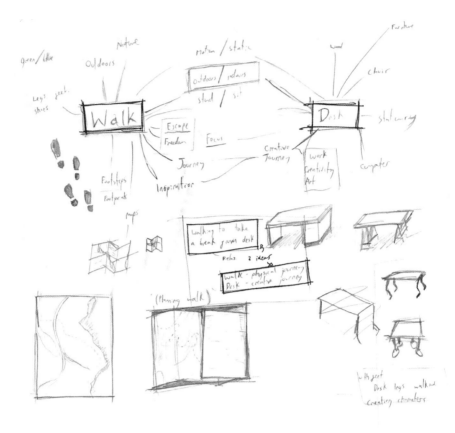

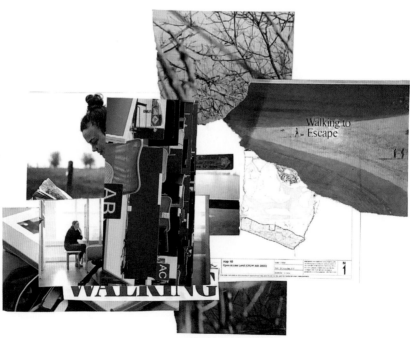

16 © Inter IKEA Systems B.V. 2010   2015-09-21   18748   AA-50-147-7

30 designdice™

Context

While every creative problem is unique, any given discipline will have established patterns of behaviour, expectations or processes that support and underpin good practice. As students, we often miss a number of these themes through lack of experience, or we ignore them as a result of bad habits. Equally, as professionals (often with significant wisdom), we can all relate to moments of creative block, or the dull persistence of routine. In short, we all have creative blind spots.

designdice™ is a creative tool that seeks to address some of these challenges by grouping loose stages of a creative process thematically by colour.[36] The set consists of 9 dice: 1 black = strategic planning; 4 red = research and context; 2 green = idea development; 1 blue = craft and production; and 1 yellow = time. Pick a suitable theme at any given moment in a project, and then roll one (or more) of the relevant dice. This presents an objective keyword prompt, inviting a series of creative responses that will encourage breadth and depth in your thinking. Every word is interpreted by you in the light of the project you're working on, so the meaning of each suggestion changes with each new context. There is a finite number of words, but (arguably) an infinite number of combinations.

Practice

Of course this is a physical tool and requires the actual set of dice to embrace their full potential. However, as an example to whet your appetite, the following exercise is just one of several thousand possible combinations. It's useful at the front end of a project, when you're in the early stages of researching a subject or looking for initial insights. Write and draw. Be as visual as you can, and externalize your thinking quickly (don't edit in your head – see the Edit Switch on pp. 116–121).

For this exercise, we'll use one of the red (research) dice plus the yellow (timer) dice. Assume you've rolled the word *map*, which is both a noun and a verb, and then the number 60, which we'll interpret as 60 minutes, although this could be seconds, hours or even days.

1 | Limiting yourself to 20 minutes, and using a current project as a base, create a two-dimensional '*map*' of your project's physical world. Spend some time collating basic data relating to your subject – people, places, signifiers, themes – and record this on a large sheet of paper or sticky notes (one thought per note). Work intuitively to begin with, and only use the knowledge you already have.

2 | Spend the next 20 minutes considering the word *map* more laterally, exploring a broader range of visual and textual expressions. For example:

• Pictorial map (consider all the visual relationships to your subject).
• Historical map (track the evolution of knowledge over time).
• Experiential map (visualize how your subject feels)... and so on.

3 | Finish by spending a final 20 minutes abstractly considering *map* – perhaps as a verb, inviting you to 'map' your subject onto other (random) elements (such as technology, education, music or politics). Force new connections or associations, and see what happens. Go with the word and interpret it as you wish – for as long as is useful. Then consider Steps 1 through 3 and identify areas for further research, key insights and potential themes for early ideas – returning to the dice as and when you have need.

Reflect

The designdice™ essentially work by giving you a tangible reference point to kick against within the context of an existing brief. Often the problem isn't the absence of possibilities, it's the presence of too much choice – we can all become paralyzed in the uncertainty of not knowing what to do next. The keyword prompt simply reduces those options and forces a reaction to a predefined (and limited) point of reference – there are only so many interpretations of the word *map* in any given context. This, in turn, creates sufficient space and confidence to take another step forward, and another, until you realize (almost without noticing it) that you are moving again.

31 The Things that Get in the Way

Helps: Identify the inhibitors to your creativity.

Time: 2–8 hours+.

Tools: Pencil, paper, sticky notes.

Context

Inevitably, when we pursue our creative interests, there are struggles, disappointments and creative blocks along the way. It's familiar ground for anyone involved in bringing innovative work to life – regardless of your age, discipline or experience. We all come up against *things* that attempt to prevent us from being creative or productive. These things, which are often intangible and invisible, are invariably generated from within. We can be our own worst enemy.

Practice

This exercise will help you to draw up a personal list of the Things that Get in the Way. More often than not, there will be a few that stand out or resonate with you in a more intuitive way (either positively or negatively), so try to lead with these. The intention here is to name anything acting as an inhibitor to your work – physically or intellectually – and whatever small steps you can take at this point will develop into giant leaps in the fullness of time. The naming brings the enemy out into the open and, when it's out in the open, you can begin to deal with it.

Part 1: Identifying the things
- Define creativity in your own terms.
- Does this reflect your existing creative practice in any way?
- How does that make you feel?
- What might you change?
- Do you view creativity as *magic* or as *commitment*?

Magic ———————————————— Commitment

- Where are you now (mark an X)?
- Where do you want to be (mark an O)?
- What do you turn to for instant gratification in general?
- What do you turn to for instant gratification in creative terms?
- Do you gravitate towards *order* or *chaos*?

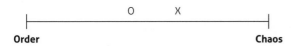

- Where are you now (mark an X)?
- Where do you want to be (mark an O)?
- Where are your obvious strengths?
- And your weaknesses (spoken and unspoken)?
- Where are your limitations (the edges of where you feel comfortable)?
- What is your creative centre of gravity?
- Who or what competes with this?

Part 2: Naming the things

1 | Define all the projects you'd like to work on (your creative bucket list). Organize them into two categories: 'The things I could start today' and 'The things for later'.

2 | What has prevented you from working on them up to now? Are there opposing forces working against these things? Try to name them. Think generic and specific.

3 | Who or what do you usually blame when things don't work (or don't start)?

4 | What do you fear (creatively)?

5 | We all procrastinate – what form does yours take (internally and externally)?

6 | Does self-sabotage feature in your practice? How?

7 | Read through your answers from Parts 1 and 2, distilling them down to a definitive summary of the Things that Get in the Way. Create an ordered list.

Part 3: Dealing with the things

This is the hard part. Sometimes an awareness of your barriers is enough to make adjustments that will limit their negative effect, so pinning your list to a wall near your workspace may be enough. However, if you wish to take this a step further, you can try the following:

Fuck resistance (or fuck the things)

Write or formally typeset your Things that Get in the Way list with the word **FUCK** (in bold, all-caps) preceding each word. Put it somewhere prominent.

Resistance fund

Sometimes a lack of funds is a limitation or barrier for a new project. Equally, accountability is a great mediator for positive change. Identify a project you'd like to resource more intentionally (perhaps from your creative bucket list above), then find a container or create a digital account to use like a swear jar, dropping some money in it each time you catch yourself doing something from your Things that Get in the Way list. Make sure the money goes only towards your designated project.

Resistance contract

Look at your creative bucket list and complete the following for as many items as necessary:

I, _____*insert name*_____

Am going to start _____ on _____ at _____

and finish by _____

Signed _____*insert signature*_____

Reflect

When it comes to fears (of failure, rejection, the unknown, of doing it wrong, being judged or evaluated, not being creative enough, not being good enough, not being rewarded for your efforts, and so on), we firmly believe that they can be overcome. While this is easier said than done, a solution is often found in consciously choosing not to worry, and deciding to begin. Forget about the outcomes, focus on the journey and enjoy the process. Driving many of these fears is the common trap of comparison with others. Whether this is through grades at school, social-media likes, achievements or behaviours, our tendency to compare ourselves with others is one of the leading causes of our unhappiness. *Choosing* not to allow social or creative comparison to influence how we feel about ourselves (or the work we do) is the essential lesson. And, seen in the light of your individual, unique perspective on the world, choosing to start is everything this resistance is trying to block.

The work of Neil Fiore, Steven Pressfield and Edward de Bono informed many of the original workshops that led to The Things that Get in the Way, and it's only right to credit them again here. If this workshop has touched a creative nerve for you, we'd highly recommend reading some of their work in more detail.[37]

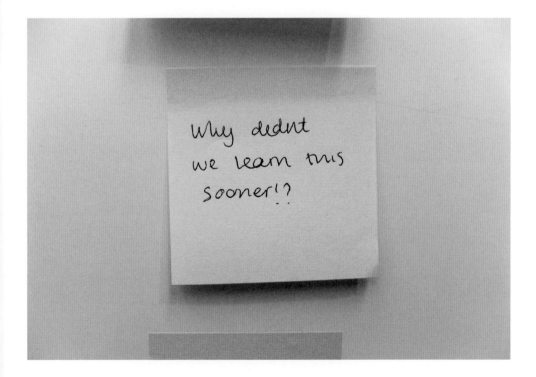

Epilogue

Make your own tools

We started this journey with a few underlying assumptions: creativity as something that we are, creativity as something that we need to encourage out into the open, and creativity as something that's best suggested rather than described. Along the way, we've considered the importance of our unique *identities*, the importance of recognizing and addressing our *habits*, and (especially as adults) the need to reconnect with risk, failure and *play* as mechanisms to enhance our creative practice. We've also explored many of these themes and ideas as practical exercises that we hope have stretched and challenged your thinking. However, at its core – for us at least – this book has been built on the premise of trying to uncover a unique creative process. Yours.

And we need to finish this work.

There are many books on creative processes. This particular one, however, is unique in that it's ultimately about *your* process, and key to its success is the translation of the external ideas you've explored into a future expression of them that is fully owned by you. The ideas have to move beyond being captured as words on a page, or your experience of them in a workshop exercise. They have to become internalized, and re-expressed. You need to make your own tools.

We've touched upon your evolving process model several times (the tangible expression of what you do, and how you do it), and many of our activities have sought to encourage the best (and worst) of this out of the shadows. In concluding, we'd like to leave you with a final challenge that seeks to fuse the most significant of these elements into a single, distinctive whole – creating a unique tool that will complement your practice from this point forward.

In a sense, this book is *our* tool – an external expression of principles that have shaped our teaching practice for years, realized in such a way that others can make use of it. We want you to make *yours*.

Part 1: Reflect

Spend some time reflecting on the experiences, challenges and ideas within the book that have resonated with you in some way (positive *and* negative), referring to any notes you may have made, or to the outputs from particular exercises. Add to this any observations you (or perhaps others) have made on the broader landscape of your creative practice.

Allow yourself time to do this. Don't rush – distil your thinking into key areas, possibly located around identity, habit or play, or other themes that emerge as you reflect. Collate your thinking in whatever way makes sense to you (although sticky notes are a great start).

1.1: Pause
1 | Gather this material and (ideally) find some space to organize it all so you can see as much of it in one go as possible.

2 | Allow yourself some time to absorb what you have before you. It's clearly not the complete you, but it will go some way to highlighting a number of things that may well be of importance in reimagining the way you wish to work.

3 | In particular, consider each theme both in isolation and holistically, noting elements to retain and areas you want to address. It's likely there will be repeating ideas and/or contradictions,

'Make your own tools. Hybridize your tools in order to build unique things. Even simple tools that are your own can yield entirely new avenues of exploration. Remember, tools amplify our capacities, so even a small tool can make a big difference.'

Bruce Mau [1]

so allowing yourself the time to reflect and absorb the material is vital at this stage.

1.2: Polarize

1 | From this collection, gather together the elements you wish to retain in your practice: historical maxims, any apparent strengths, things that make you unique, elements you'd hate to lose, helpful words or language, useful ideas or thinking, and so on.

2 | Next, gather together the things that need addressing or considering anew: any blind spots, flaws, bad habits, negative voices, omissions, surprises, alternatives, and so on. You may need to amend, react to or invert what's already there to clearly articulate these areas.

Opposite (Top): Thinking cube by Ben White (tool as a physical object)

(Lower): Design process blueprint by Carolyn Browse (tool as a visual diagram)

Below: TRACK process game by Kira Gardner and Olivia Moores (tool as an activity)

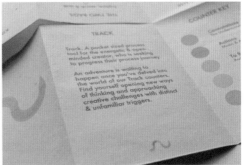

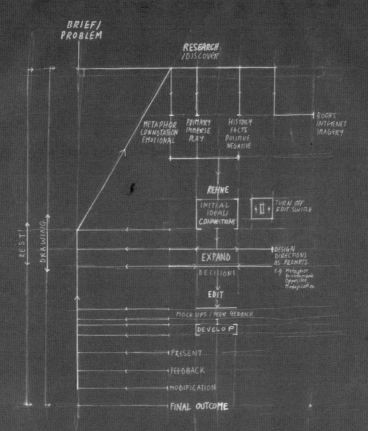

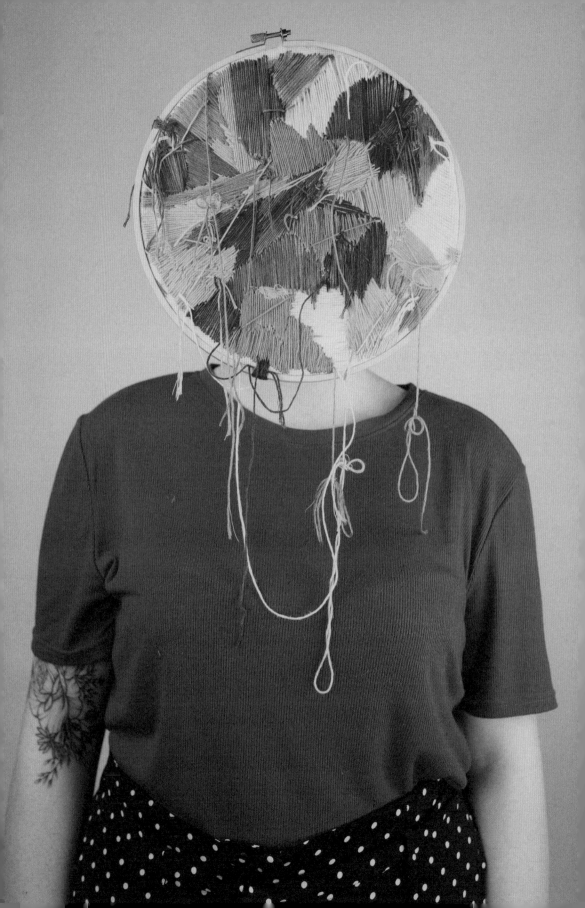

Part 2: Create

Consider these unique-to-you themes in the light of your current creative process, and distil them into a unique creative *tool* that can be used by the *future you* (or other students, professionals, educators) to enhance your practice and embody these principles. Embrace and enhance the positives, acknowledge and address the negatives, challenge, provoke and ultimately harness your inner potential. The tool could range from a simple visual prompt that succinctly summarizes a key idea or action, to a more involved mantra or process diagram you wish to live and/or create by. Beyond this, it could be a game or experience, or a complex system that requires an instruction manual, a PhD and plenty of time. It could be 2D, 3D or 4D. It could be physical or virtual. There are no real limitations.

Its success will be measured against how likely it is to inspire you (and others) to continually better yourself and find a more vibrant, holistic and productive expression of your creativity. It has to work in real terms – provoking you when you are tired, frustrated or tempted to pick the easy route. It has to have metaphorical (or even literal) teeth!

The aim is to express the future you in a way that is meaningful to your practice, and in a form that you can refer back to regularly. Your best tools will evolve from a thorough and honest reflection of your needs. We've included a few examples from our workshops to help orientate your thinking and get you going, but don't lean too heavily on these. Adapt and own the reflections you've collated from the previous chapters into a tool that challenges and provokes *you*, and you'll find a better version of your creative self every time you sit down to make something new.

So, another book on creativity – which ends by defining yours.

Notes

Introduction

1   Robert Doisneau, *Robert Doisneau: Retrospective* (The Photographers Gallery, 1982)
2   Nicola Salkeld & Ashley Rudolph (quoting Stefan Boufler), *In the Face of Death* (https://moth.org.uk/In-The-Face-of-Death_Publication)
3   David Mamet, *On Directing Film*, Penguin Books, 1992

Chapter 1: Identity

1   Richard Rohr, *Falling Upward*, Jossey-Bass, 2011
2   Brian Eno, *A Year with Swollen Appendices*, Faber and Faber, 1996
3   Aristotle, *original source unknown*
4   Rob Bell, *What We Talk About When We Talk About God*, Harper Collins, 2013
5   Neil Fiore, *The Now Habit*, TarcherPerigee, 2007
6   Sun Tzu, *The Art of War* (multiple translations)
7   Steven Pressfield, *The War of Art*, Black Irish Entertainment, 2012
8   Neil Fiore, *op. cit.*
9   Saul Bass, *original source unknown*
10 Henry Moore, *original source unknown*
11 Often attributed to Michelangelo (or John Ruskin, or George F. Pentecost... https://quoteinvestigator.com/2014/06/22/chip-away/)
12 Pablo Picasso, quoted in 'Modern Living: Osmosis in Central Park', *Time*, October 4, 1976
13 Michael Wolff (https://www.brainpickings.org/2011/03/28/michael-wolff-creativity-visual-life)

Chapter 2: Habit

1   Twyla Tharp, *The Creative Habit*, Simon & Schuster, 2006
2   Charles Duhigg, *The Power of Habit*, Random House, 2014
3   Shaun McNiff, *Trust the Process*, Shambhala Publications Inc., 1998
4   Thomas Moore, *Care of the Soul*, Piatkus, 2012
5   Mason Currey (quoting Nicholson Baker), *Daily Rituals: How Artists Work*, Penguin Random House, 2013
6   Brian Christian & Tom Griffiths, *Algorithms to Live By*, Macmillan, 2016
7   Silvio Lorusso, *Entreprecariat: Everyone Is an Entrepreneur. Nobody Is Safe*, Onomatopee, 2019

8   Daniel Kahneman, *Thinking, Fast and Slow*, Farrar, Straus & Giroux, 1994
9   Dorothea Brande, *Becoming a Writer*, orig. published 1934, Macmillan reprint, 1996
10 John Cleese, 'Open mode & closed mode' (speech delivered to Video Arts conference in 1991)
11 Often attributed to Ernest Hemingway (but also to Gowan McGland and Dylan Thomas) https://quoteinvestigator.com/2016/09/21/write-drunk/)
12 James Webb Young, *A Technique for Producing Ideas*, McGraw-Hill, 1965
13 Friedrich Nietzsche, *Beyond Good and Evil*, orig. published 1886, Aziloth Books edition, 2010
14 Warren Motte (quoting Raymond Queneau), *Oulipo: A Primer of Potential Literature*, Dalkey Archive Press, 1998
15 Raymond Queneau, *Into the Maze: OULIPO* (https://poets.org/text/maze-oulipo)
16 Raymond Queneau, *op. cit.*

Chapter 3: Play

1   Johan Huizinga (quoting Plato), *Homo Ludens: A Study of the Play Element in Culture*, Maurice Temple Smith Ltd, 1970
2   Teresa Amabile et al, 'Social Influences on Creativity: The Effects of Contracted-For Reward', in *Journal of Personality and Social Psychology*, Vol. 50, 1986
3   Peter Gray, *Free to Learn*, Basic Books, 2015
4   Paul Weiner, *Creativity and Beyond*, SUNY Press, 2000
5   Max Delbrück, *The Principle of 'limited sloppiness'* (http://www.datadeluge.com/2010/08/principle-of-limited-sloppiness.html)
6   Patrick Bateson & Paul Martin, *Play, Playfulness, Creativity and Innovation*, Cambridge University Press, 2013
7   Ric Knowles, *Improvisation* (Canadian theatre review, https://ctr.utpjournals.press/doi/10.3138/ctr.143.3)
8   Brian Eno & Peter Schmidt, *Oblique Strategies*, Opal, 1975
9   Sally Jenkinson (quoting Friedrich von Schiller), *Genius of Play: Celebrating the Spirit of Childhood*, Hawthorn Press, 2001
10 Daniel Cable, *Alive at Work: The Neuroscience of Helping Your People Love What They Do*, Harvard Business Review Press, 2018

11 Jaak Panksepp, *Affective Neuroscience*, Oxford University Press, 1998

12 Mihaly Csikszentmihalyi, *Flow*, Harper Perennial Modern Classics, 1992

13 Suzanne Held & Marek Špinka, 'Animal play and animal welfare', in *Animal Behaviour*, Vol. 81, Issue 5, May 2011

14 Michael Schrage, *Serious Play*, Harvard Business Review Press, 1999

15 Patrick Bateson & Paul Martin, *op. cit.*

16 *Ibid.*

Chapter 4: Practice

1 If you are curious about your wider personality and strengths, search for the Myers-Briggs, StrengthsFinder or Enneagram tests online.

2 Paul Thek, 'Teaching Notes', 1978–1981, Cooper Union School of Arts

3 Part 1 is based on 'Who, Me?' by Rochelle Feinstein, in *Draw It with Your Eyes Closed: The Art of the Art Assignment*, Paper Monument, 2012

4 Chuck Palahniuk, *Fight Club*, W. W. Norton & Company, 1996

5 Anthony Stevens, *On Jung*, Routledge, 1990

6 How many uses for a paper-clip can you think of in 5 minutes? *Source unknown.*

7 Edward de Bono, *Six Thinking Hats*, Penguin Life, 2016

8 https://en.wikipedia.org/wiki/Desire_path

9 James Webb Young, *A Technique for Producing Ideas*, McGraw-Hill, 1965

10 Benjamin Baird et al, 'Inspired by Distraction', in *Psychological Science*, vol. 23, no. 10, 2012, pp. 1117–1122

11 Steve Jobs, *I, Steve: Steve Jobs in his Own Words*, Hardie Grant Books, 2011

12 Don Koberg, *The Universal Traveller*, W. Kaufmann, 1974

13 Virginia Woolf, *Genius and Ink: Virginia Woolf on How to Read*, TLS Books, 2019

14 Jean-Claude Carrière & Umberto Eco, *This is Not the End of the Book: A Conversation*, Vintage, 2011

15 Nathaniel Kleitman, 'Ultradian Rhythms', in *Journal of Sleep Research & Sleep Medicine*, Vol 5; 4

16 Francesco Cirillo, *Pomodoro Technique* (https://francescocirillo.com/pages/pomodoro-technique)

17 Neil Fiore, *The Now Habit*, TarcherPerigee, 2007

18 Haruki Murakami interviewed by John Wray, 'The Art of Fiction No. 182', in *The Paris Review*, issue 170, Summer 2004

19 Jay Rubin, *Haruki Murakami and the Music of Words*, Vintage, 2005

20 Ann Charlotte Thorsted , *Play – To Create and to Live*, International DesignCamp, 2013

21 Hunter S. Thompson speaking with Charlie Rose, *The Charlie Rose Show*, PBS, June 13, 1997

22 Agnes Martin, 'Beauty Is the Mystery of Life' (essay based on lecture given at Carnegie Museum of Art, Pittsburgh, 1989)

23 Phil Carter of Carter Wong (1984–2016) and Carter Studio (2016–present, https://carterstudio.co.uk/)

24 Melinda Wenner (quoting Gordon M. Burghardt), 'The Serious Need for Play', in *Scientific American Mind*, vol. 20, no. 1, Feb 2009

25 Erlend Loe, *Naïve. Super*, Canongate Books, 2001

26 Design Council (https://www.designcouncil.org.uk/news-opinion/what-framework-innovation-design-councils-evolved-double-diamond and also https://www.designcouncil.org.uk/resources/guide/beyond-net-zero-systemic-design-approach)

27 Directed by Thomas Riedelsheimer, *Rivers and Tides*, Skyline Productions, 2001

28 Andy Goldsworthy, *source unkown*

29 Andy Merrifield, *The Amateur*, Verso, 2018

30 The Elephant Juggling Bicycles picture is one we've used for years, but we can't remember (or find) its source. We may have made it up in a random moment of educational spontaneity, or (more likely) it may have originated elsewhere and we've just adopted it. Either way, it serves the purpose of creating a random concept, for which we will all have our own visual mental picture. If you are the original author, we thank you!

31 Nancy Skolos & Thomas Wedell, *Graphic Design Process: From Problem to Solution*, Laurence King Publishing, 2012

32 James Webb Young, *op. cit.*

33 Steven Johnson, *Where Good Ideas Come From*, Penguin, 2010

34 Carl Jung, *Psychological Types*, Rascher Verlag, 1921

35 Mark Twain, *Mark Twain's Own Autobiography*, University of Wisconsin Press, 2010

36 Andy Neal, http://www.designdice.co.uk (Wild Goose-Media Ltd)

37 Neil Fiore, *op cit.*; Steven Pressfield, *The War of Art*, Black Irish Entertainment, 2012; Edward de Bono, *Lateral Thinking* and *Six Thinking Hats* (both Penguin Life, 2016).

Epilogue

1 Bruce Mau, *Incomplete Manifesto for Growth* (https://www.massivechangenetwork.com/bruce-mau-manifesto)

Index

Acknowledgements

For Kate and Helena.

Thanks to...
The students who participated in our
Disruption, *Generator* and *Persona* workshops
in both the UK and Germany. You taught us
so much and we are eternally grateful for
your enthusiasm and commitment to some
very early and (at the time) questionable
workshops (*Warrior Mode v1* anyone...?); Estie
Adamczyk, Yehya Al-Hafidh, Orest Balunnik,
Sabine Banner, Sophie Bohne, Lucy Bristow,
Kirsty Carrington, Samuel Clothier, Draig
Conybear, Amy Cuttle, Lily Dempsey, Lydia
Ellawand, Alessandro Ferrari, Georgia Foote,
Zoe Foster, Izzy Galloway, Kira Gardner, Gina
Glaso, Amelia Hackett, Annie Haines, Sophie
Hare, Sophie Harper, Rebecca Hawkey,
Rosanna Highton, Andrew Hodgkiss, Sabrina
Holtz, Charlotte Hope, Clare Ince, Chris Ireland,
Frankie Jackson, Rebecca James, Jenny Jeon,
Emily Kane, Sina Keller, Gino Kellner, Daniel
Kraska, Mathew Leong, Rowan Lewis, Hannah
Li, Jeremy Liu, Bettina Mader, Chandler
Massey, Manuela Maurus, Rebecca Mayne, Eve
McConnell, Christian Merk, Dan Moggs, Olivia
Moore, Carolin Münch, Dan Murphy, Sebastian
Nitsche, Alice O'Toole, Victoria Onaiyekan,
Rachel Potter, Ellie Powell, Joseph Privett,
Chloe Rendells, Luke Robinson, Keira Rowe,
Tom Rule, Zach Rush, Jessie Russell, Sonja
Salko, Franziska Schneider, Artjom Schneider,
Eleanor Smith, Nicholas Smith, Amir Steinberg,
Isabella Stoll, Matthias Weißenböck, Ben
White, Tasha Williams, Walter Wunderlich,
Judy Zhubau and Raphael Zöschinger.

Jon Unwin, Nikki Salkeld, Ashley Rudolph,
Steve Bond, Lizzie Ridout, Steve House, Chris
Topf and Stefan Bufler for championing us
from the sidelines at Falmouth University
(and beyond). Your support and encouragement
have been a lifeline in often dangerous and
uncharted academic waters.

Jocelyn Affleck, Anthea Moys and Phil Carter
for your conversations, workshop ideas and
extracts from your sketchbooks.

Kara Hattersley-Smith at Laurence King for first
believing in the project and giving us the chance
to let it grow. Liz Faber for guiding us through
the complexity of bringing a book to life and for
teaching us how to edit. Allan Sommerville for
giving our words and ideas a visual voice and
dealing with designers as clients (surely the
worst possible combination...?). And to James
Buswell for quietly managing the production
of the project from afar.

Finally, all the individuals who generously
contributed visual material to the book: Jocelyn
Affleck, Maria Beardall, Daisy Bourne, Carolyn
Browse, Millie Burdon, Henry Carrow, Phil Carter,
Draig Conybear, Hannah De Oliveira Whitlock,
Nicole Ellis, Kira Gardner, Annie Haines, Tom
Heath, Dan Hiscock, Steve House, Chris Ireland,
Tom Jenkins, Taylor Jones, Abbie Macphail,
Kyra Marks, Nina Masterton, Justas Matkevicius,
Rebecca Mayne, Dan Moggs, Olivia Moores,
River Orrey, Ellie Powell, Lizzie Ridout, Ashley
Rudolph, Bethany Rush, Zach Rush, Eleanor
Smith, Juliana Smith, Chris Topf and Ben White.

Image creators are credited within the main
body of the book. All other material by Andy
Neal and Dion Star. If we have missed you or
misquoted you – blame ~~Andy. No, blame Dion.
No Andy. No Dion~~...